On a Chicken Wing and a Prayer

Cover design by Sara Young

ISBN: 978-1-960678-91-1   1 2 3 4 5 6 7 8 9 10

Printed in the United States of America

Lori Allison Metzger

On a Chicken Wing and a Prayer

A Mother/Daughter's
Journey from Addiction
to Redemption

DEDICATION

I want to say thank you to my family for loving me, encouraging me, and not giving up on me finishing, even when I quit 100 times!!

To my grandson Noah, the one who loves me to the moon and back....my honey from the rock. The sweetest thing that came out of the hardest place of my life.

To my dad & mom, Jim and Angela Allison, thank you for showing me Jesus because I would not have made it through this tough time without Him.

To my four daughters, Lindy, Kristin, Eden, and Mary Kathryn thank you for the tears, laughter, and love.... we made it through some stuff!!!

I love you all big!!

Contents

Acknowledgments

First of all, I want to give all the glory, honor, and praise to Jesus the only one who made redemption even possible. Thank you for your unfailing love and for never giving up on me or my daughter. Thank you for using our story to bring hope to others.

I would like to express my sincere gratitude to my editor Donna Mosher for her expertise in providing guidance and encouragement, even pushing me to make the book better and to keep going.

A special thanks to John Schondelmayer at Four Rivers Publishing for seeing it as a ministry of hope and not just a book.

To Sarah Petelle at Four Rivers Publishing, I say thank you for coaching me through the publishing process and for putting up with my tons of questions and emails. Thanks to everyone at Four Rivers Publishing who played a part in doing the hard work to turn this manuscript into a book.

I want to thank my friends, Editor Carol Mann and Author Kendra Roehl for helping to proofread and edit in the early stages of starting the book and encouraging me to keep writing because they believe in the hope of our story.

A big thank you to my dear friend & sister in Christ, Toni Mason who took up the task of proofreading and cheering me on when I felt weary.

I say thank you to my friend Kim Welch, who has encouraged me through the process of writing the book and even lost a little sleep at the end by helping me finish a few changes three days before the deadline to turn the manuscript into the publisher.

There are those who gave finances and others encouragement throughout this whole journey, from praying Eden back to Jesus to the last sentence in this book. I could never say thank you enough!

I can't put into words all that's in my heart to say thank you to my daughter Eden. Thank you for being vulnerable and open to share the failures and triumphs of your personal journey through addiction. For hanging in there with me and putting on paper your thoughts, feelings and memories of what was happening in your life during these difficult times. Thank you for helping to make this book complete.

Last but not least I say thank you to my family who believed in me, stood by me and who probably wished they had a dime for every time they heard me say "I can't, I have to work on the book!". Lindy thank you for adding to those jail cell tales.

From the bottom of my heart, I love and thank you all.

Introduction

"THESE PEOPLE"

*M*ark 8 tells a story of Jesus feeding 4,000 people. The disciples asked Jesus this question. . . . How can we find enough bread to feed these people in this desolate place?

Jesus and His disciples were in Decapolis, an area Jews avoided because it was Gentile territory. But Jesus cared about "these people" and where they had come from saying, "Some of them have come a long distance." We don't know the distance some people have traveled to come to Jesus. We don't know the pain, the struggle it took them to get there. It is important as Christ followers to extend grace.

Jesus is letting us know that the Bread of Life is for all people in all places. We don't get to pick and choose who we hand it out to! It's sad to think that we ever thought we could. Jesus said, "Freely you have received; freely give." (Matthew 10:8)

I am sad and broken to admit that for me, before 2011, "drug addicts" would have fallen into the category of "these people," the "lowlifes". Until my own daughter, Eden, became one of "these people"!! Jesus showed me how to love others through my daughter getting caught in the chains of addiction. I realized as a follower of Christ, I was failing. I don't have enough to love "these people" that I always thought I was somehow above!! I will never have enough if it stays in my hands. If it's in my hands I am in control. But when I put it in Jesus' hands, that's where the miracle happens.

When the disciples gave the bread to Jesus, what did He do? He took it, He blessed it, and He broke it. The multiplication happened in the disciples' hands after Jesus gave it back to them. When I put my life and my situation in God's hands, that's exactly what He did. . . . He took me, He broke me, and He blessed me. Not to destroy me, but so that my story would give hope to somebody else.

The cool thing is there were leftovers!! There were seven baskets of bread left after all 4,000 people there that day had full bellies. I have plenty left to share! Seven is the number of completion. Jesus loves and gave Himself for ALL people.

When you go through a time of breaking, look what's in your basket and remind yourself that He is able!!

My prayer is, "Oh God, let me never forget!!!" Don't forget what He's already done!!!

Elizabeth Elliot wrote, "If my life is broken when given to Jesus, it may be because pieces will feed a multitude when a loaf would satisfy only a little boy."[1]

Out of my brokenness, I write this story to share the blessing of hope.

---

1   https://oneragamuffin.com/tag/elisabeth-elliot/

CHAPTER 1

Our Edie Bug

"Children are a heritage from the Lord."
—Psalm 127:3

LIFE UNRAVELING

Drugs, gangs, and murder. Why are there detectives in my living room? How did we get here? They introduced themselves as detectives from the Mobile Police Department Homicide Division and they asked to speak to my daughter Eden.

As they began to talk of gangs, drugs, and murder, questions raced through my mind: *Where is my daughter? Is she dead? What's happening?* I knew Eden had been on a rebellious road for a while and I had been praying for her for three years, but I never imagined that those prayers would be answered in this way. Desperation has a sound, and for me it was the sound of hearing my own heartbeat in my ears as I sat in my living room answering

questions for the detectives. I felt like I couldn't hear myself think above the sound of my beating heart as fear flooded my body while the detectives explained to me that they were looking for Eden. To tell you the truth, I wish I could make sense of it all, but I had no idea just how chaotic things were about to get in our lives. But before we can get to the end, we must start at the beginning with the birth of my third daughter, Eden, in 1990.

FRUITFUL AND BLESSED

Elizabeth "Eden" Metzger was born April 2, 1990, in Mobile, Alabama. She looked just like her dad, who gave her the name Eden, which means "fruitful". What a beautiful name for our precious daughter. The day before we came home from the hospital, Steve had gone to Party City and apparently bought every pink baby sign and banner that he could find and covered our yard, mailbox, and front door. As we drove home from the hospital and pulled into our driveway our house looked like "here's your sign".... "It's A Girl" was everywhere!

Nine months earlier, on the day we found out we were pregnant with Eden, Steve was inside out of himself. He told every person he met that day . . . from everybody at his dental appointment to some random lady in line at the grocery store, even the cashier—that we were going to have a baby. Why all this excitement? Let me explain.

Several years before I met Steve, he had been married and had fertility issues. During this time, he sought medical help and had been told by physicians that he would never be able to father a child. He could not accept this news, so he underwent major surgery to correct the problem, only to be told that it was unsuccessful. Before we were married, he explained all this to me and told me that he could not have children. So, this was his miracle day. God is not confined by the limits of our doctors or even our own bodies. At age thirty-four, Steve would finally get to experience fatherhood from conception to delivery.

He had already taken to being "Dad" to my two little girls, Lindy, five, and Kristin, three, who were born from my first marriage. But it would be our daughter, Eden, that would connect us all to make us one family.

With Lindy and Kristin, her two older sisters, or should I say "little mamas" ready to take over, she became our "Edie Bug", a nickname her dad gave her.

Before we knew it, she was walking and talking. She had a cute little raspy voice and was an entertainer from the start. Eden kept us all laughing. Right before her second birthday, we had our fourth and final baby, Mary Kathryn. Even though they were only twenty-one months apart, Eden took to her like she was now the "little mama". I think Eden thought she was her real-life baby doll. Mary Kathryn became Eden's shadow and wanted to do everything she did.

One day when Eden was around two years old, she was sitting in her high chair waiting for me to get her lunch ready. She was hungry, or should I say "hangry" (when you're so hungry, you're angry). In her cute little raspy voice, she began to say the same phrase over and over . . . "want hot arrff, want hot arrff."

I could not understand what she was trying to say, so I started guessing. The more I guessed wrong, the more frustrated she got. Finally, it hit me. I remembered that she called dogs "arrffs". Eden wanted a "hot arrff" . . . a hot dog! She looked up with a big smile on her face. I had finally guessed it right.

Eden was my little Tom Boy. She loved bugs, all kinds of bugs, so "Edie Bug" became the perfect nickname for her. Playing in dirt and looking for bugs were her life. I think a cup of roly-polies could entertain her all day. Being unafraid of anything, she would catch little green lizards and clip them to her ears like earrings. One day she had a lizard clamped onto one of her ears and it would not let go. She came running inside with the lizard still dangling from her ear and wanted me to help her get it off. First of all, I don't touch lizards, and secondly, I was suddenly faced with the potential of the thing getting loose in my house! I frantically said, "Mama can't do that, honey, go look in the bathroom mirror and figure it out!" Lucky for Eden, her grandmother—whom we call "Mamaw"—happened to be visiting us that day and helped her get the lizard unclamped from her ear. Mamaw is my Mom, and where this bravery for her to touch a lizard came from that day, I have no clue. I have vivid memories from my childhood of the same woman standing in a chair, screaming and swinging a broom while trying to kill a roach. But it seems something magical takes over us when we have grandkids. With the lizard detached, a smile of relief came over Eden's face, but it didn't stop her from doing it again.

I don't like "creepy crawly creatures", so she did not get her love for bugs from me. As she got older and one of those creatures appeared in our house, I would scream, "Eden, I'll pay you, please come get it!!" I could always count on "Edie Bug".

KICKIN' IT FOR JESUS

All four of my girls loved to sing and entertain. When Eden was around four years old, a friend of mine who was a Methodist pastor invited my girls to come sing at his church. They had practiced for a few weeks, and then came the big day. They were all dressed alike in their home-made matching dresses. They still hold those outfits against me, along with those humongous hair bows that they say were "big enough to put cricks in our necks." I think it's a southern thing. Maybe that's why we have so many chiropractors in the south.

My little girls (top row: Kristin and Lindy, bottom row: Mary Kathryn and Eden).

We arrived at the church early and the Pastor ushered us in and had us seated on the front row. Right before the message, the Pastor called my girls up on the stage to sing their song, *He's Still Working On Me.* They sang the first verse. Everything was going well, but as they began to sing the chorus, *He's still working on me to make me what I ought to be. It took Him just a week to make the moon and the stars, the sun and the earth and Jupiter and Mars. How loving and patient He must be, He's still working on me,* Eden began to kick her leg up to the beat of the music. She kicked so high we could see her panties! The congregation began to snicker—even I could barely hold back my laughter. I was on the front row now trying to make that "big" eye contact with her to give her that "mama look", shaking my head "no" and mouthing "stop." It was useless; she was in her own world doing her own thing. It seemed the more we laughed the more she felt the need to entertain. A star was born, or at least, the family comedian.

SCHOOL DAYS

Not only was she cute and funny, but she was smart. A few months after she started K-5 at Knollwood Christian School, her dad and I separated. We were living in Theodore, Alabama at the time. We moved out of our home and went to stay with my parents in Florida. My husband Steve, Eden's dad, had a lot of great attributes. He was one of the most giving people I had ever known. He was a rather shy person with a dry sense of humor. He was a hard worker, supported, and even spoiled our family. Yet one big problem stood in the way of ours being a happy home. Steve was an alcoholic. This was one of those times that moving out of our home was a way to avoid the chaos of alcoholism. It was tough on all of us.

This was a hard move for Eden because it was her first year in school and she was comfortable and had lots of friends in the small private Christian school she attended in Mobile, Alabama. Her two older sisters had been attending this school for several years and I did a lot of volunteering there and took Eden with me. Also, the school was affiliated and located at the church we attended. Between school and church, we were there so much that this place was like home to my kids.

But for the time being, we left and stayed in Florida. I didn't know how long that would be, so I had to enroll the girls in school. Eden cried, but mainly because she wanted to sit by her only friend, a little girl that she knew from the church that we attended where my dad was the pastor. This was the only little girl Eden knew in this town. We were already going through enough adjustments, so for now, I let her "drop out" and decided to keep her at home with me. To say it in formal terms, I withdrew her. K-5 was optional because attending school was not mandatory until first grade.

Three months later over the Christmas school break, we left my parents' house in Florida and moved back home with Steve in Alabama. I wanted desperately for Steve to get help and save our marriage. Although the girls loved staying with their grandparents, they were happy to be back home and with their friends at their old school. Eden picked right back up in K-5 like she hadn't even missed.

Second grade was another story. She kept coming home with all this homework to do.

So, I made an appointment with the principal. I explained about all the papers being sent home and that we pay way too much money for this school, and Eden spends way too many hours here to bring so much homework home. I reasoned that they are at school all day and need a break. I feel too much homework robs them of their free time to just be kids.

It turned out this was not homework; it was Eden's classwork because she wasn't getting it done at school.

"I don't know what's going on," I said to the principal, "but I want y'all to do whatever needs to be done for her to get her classwork done at school." My request was met with an unexpected explanation as to why Eden didn't finish her classwork at school. She was being a busybody, just walking around the classroom visiting, entertaining, and doing whatever else she wanted to do.

One day when the teacher was out of the room, she took the stuff out of her desk and moved it into an empty desk by her best friend. She figured if they weren't going to move her, she would just move herself.

She helped other students get their work done but wasn't doing her own. To try to solve the problem, they moved Eden and her desk into the hallway for a while where she was expected to sit and do her work, with less distractions.

This teacher was young; it was her first year. I'm sorry to say that she quit after that first year. Being a teacher can be tough. Things were starting to get a little worrisome because Eden's first-grade teacher had also quit after the end of her year with my angel. Eden was sweet, just a little on the active side. I know if you're a teacher, you're probably thinking . . . "Yeah, that's what all parents say." All kidding aside, we did support our teachers and taught our girls to be respectful to their teachers and they received consequences at home if they didn't.

ARMOR OF GOD

We had this routine. Every day on the way to school, we would sing this song about putting on the Armor of God that Paul talks about in Ephesians 6. Eden was about seven and Mary Kathryn was five. On this particular morning, Mary Kathryn woke up a little on the grouchy side. So as we were getting ready to sing our song, Mary Kathryn folded her arms and said, "I'm not singing, I don't want to put it on." Eden looks over at her with this serious look on her face and calmly says, "Well do you wanna go naked?" At the time I just laughed, but I thought later about the amount of truth in that statement. How often as Christians do we walk around naked with no protection from the enemy because we were weren't willing to put on the armor of God.

SWEET SALVATION

It was during these elementary years at the age of eight that Eden attended church camp where she gave her heart to Jesus. I was so excited when she came home with that news. I, too, had given my heart to Jesus at age eight. As a mom, my prayer and heart's desire for my girls was always that they would know Jesus. Naturally, the news of Eden accepting the precious gift of sweet salvation made my heart soar. Thank you, Jesus!

Eden grew in her walk with the Lord and brought others with her. She was very active in our children's church and on up through the youth group. Eden would eventually become the one at youth camp laying hands on kids and praying for them. She was a peacemaker, a kind soul, and always had a heart to help and a heart to give.

SWITCHED AT BIRTH?

As the elementary school years continued, Eden did get better at getting her work done and staying in her seat. It was her fifth-grade year that we discovered just how special others thought our Edie Bug was too. We received a letter from Duke University stating she had scored very well on a national test that she had taken at her school. The university wanted her in a program that they had specifically designed for students like Eden.

When Steve got home from work that day, I said, "Sweetie, I have some bad news." "What is it?" he asked. My reply was "I don't know how to tell you this, but I don't think we're Eden's real parents."

Looking perplexed he said, "What?" I repeated, "I don't think we're Eden's real parents." He said, "What are you talking about?" I said, "Today we received a letter from Duke University stating that they want Eden in their program because she is so smart. So, that means you must not be the daddy, and I definitely can't be the mama! She must have been switched at birth!" We had a good laugh. After checking into the program, we chose not to sign her up. Nothing against the program, we just felt it would not have been beneficial for her at that time.

ONTO MIDDLE SCHOOL AND HIGH SCHOOL

Eden entered middle school pretty much as the "Class Clown" but continued to do well with her schoolwork. As a matter of fact, she got a certificate for Entertainer of The Year (Best Sense of Humor) at her school in eighth grade. It was her nature to have fun, but not at others' expense. She was a very kind, helpful soul who wanted everyone to get along. Although very entertaining, she was not a rule-breaker by temperament. She was very respectful toward us as her parents as well as her teachers and got along well with both.

She was very active and involved in school. She did cheer-leading, basketball, and played on the softball team. I was looking through some old boxes the other day and came across her eighth-grade report card, and inside it, her English teacher had written, "There is never a dull moment when Eden is around. She lights up a room with her wit and joyful outlook on life. She also has the serious desire to serve and honor God."

Eden was a "happy-go-lucky" girl. She was a leader—very well-liked and accepted—because she was kind and accepting of others. She loved going to the beach and horseback riding. She took riding lessons for a little stint. Steve's dad—we call him Papoo—had a horse arena in Birmingham, Alabama. When we took our girls for a visit, it was no time before they were running to that arena to get on those horses.

There is never a dull moment when Eden is around. She lights up a room with her wit and joyful outlook on life. She also has the serious desire to serve and honor God.

Starting high school was an adjustment. All she had ever known was this small private school and now she was headed to a large public school. The school she had been at since K-5 did not have a high school. Her older sister, Kristin, was there to help show her the ropes. She began to get a little shy, but she continued to do well in school and be involved. She had been on a swim team when she was younger at a local swim and racket club where we were members, so she picked that back up in high school and joined the swim team. Eden rode to school every morning with her sister, Kristin. They talked about Jesus and would listen to praise and worship music on the way to school, but knowing her sister, I'm sure there was a little Britney Spears thrown in there, too. Eden had never given us any trouble; she was so much fun to be around. It was truly a joy to be her mom and to have her in our family. She kept us busy through years on the swim team, softball, basketball, cheerleading, taekwondo, and church youth group. We loved our "Edie Bug".

CHAPTER 2

Rebellion Takes a Root

Do not be misled: "Bad company corrupts good character."
Come back to your senses as you ought, and stop sinning...
—1 CORINTHIANS 15:33

REBELLIOUS FRIENDS

As Eden entered her high school years, all was good for quite some time. Eden was really close to her sister Kristin, who was three years older than her. Kristin was a very positive influence in Eden's life. They spent a lot of time hanging out with friends from the youth group at our church. The youth would all come over to our house, play games, eat, and swim. When Eden got to high school, she rode to school every day with Kristin. When Eden started her sophomore year, Kristin moved all the way across the United States to attend Bible College in Minnesota. I didn't realize at the time how devastating this was to Eden, and at such a crucial age. Eden had mainly hung out with Kristin and her friends and was now left to find her own way and sadly, lost her way. She continued to go to the youth group at our church and started hanging with people who were not good influences on her. Slowly "friends" became way too important. You know that age when they think their friends now know everything and their parents know nothing? Unfortunately, we had arrived at that point. Following her friends became more important than obeying her parents.

Parents, take caution. It is possible to be in the right church with the wrong people. Not everyone who attends your church loves Jesus. I'm not saying to "look for the perfect church." There is no perfect church. I remember my dad saying, "If you find the perfect church, don't go there, because you'll ruin it." There are no perfect churches and no perfect people. What I am trying to say is, seek the Lord and choose your friends wisely, even at church. Please understand me, the church is for broken people, but we need to use wisdom and be steadfast in our faith while ministering to others.

It's important for your children not to be "unequally yoked" in friendships, as well as marriage. The Apostle Paul said, "Do not be yoked together with unbelievers. For what do righteousness and wickedness have in common? Or what fellowship can light have with darkness? . . . What does a believer have in common with an unbeliever?" (2 Corinthians 6:14-15) I'm not saying that all these kids were unbelievers or did not know Jesus. I am saying Eden and the friends she was hanging with at this time were not following Jesus and they were not good for each other.

I can see now that her dad's absence due to alcohol addiction and separation was affecting her life. He wasn't really present in her life to give her guidance. He was never much of a disciplinarian, either. God created us to have a mom and a dad; we need the love, guidance, discipline, and nurture from both. I never doubted that he loved our kids—it's just the fact that alcohol addiction is a type of sickness that affects and robs every part of your life, and that includes your family. You can't be drunk and be an effective dad.

SATAN HAS A PLAN FOR YOUR LIFE

Satan is the enemy of our soul who desires to ruin the lives of our children and wipe out the plan God has for their lives. "The thief comes only to steal, and kill and destroy," (John 10:10). And that is the enemy's only plan for your children.

What started as small steps of rebellion ended in giant leaps.

I had heard all my life that "God has a plan for your life," but it was during this time that God began to show me that so does Satan; as a matter of fact, Ephesians tells us that he has an exact method of how he plans to achieve this destruction. We read in Ephesians to "Put on the whole armor of God, that you may be able to stand against the wiles of the devil." (6:11, NKJV) The Greek word for "wiles" is "methodia." According to Strong's, it means to follow up by a method and settled plan.

So began our battle for Eden's soul. I had already been dealing with my oldest daughter, Lindy, who had been in addiction for several years. Eden had two older sisters, Lindy and Kristin. Lindy was imprisoned in the chains of addiction and Kristin had moved to Minnesota and was attending Bible College on her way to becoming a licensed therapist. Unfortunately, Lindy would soon become an influence in Eden's life.

As I said before, this new friend group that Eden was with at church was not good for her, and she was not good for them. These parents were trying to raise their kids in church for Jesus, all the while the enemy was working hard to get them to choose the wrong path.

My goal for my children while raising them was that they would know, love, and serve Jesus and understand His love for them. Eden seemed to start to lose interest in living for Jesus. What started as small steps of rebellion ended in giant leaps.

FROM SKIPPING CHURCH TO SHOPLIFTING

This new group of church friends started hanging with some kids who weren't in church and didn't share the same convictions. It was then that Eden was introduced to marijuana and began to smoke weed. These church-going teenagers began skipping Wednesday night church. I would find out later that as soon as I dropped Eden off at youth service, she would sneak off with these friends and return just in time for me to pick her up, leading me to believe she was at church the whole time. The adults either had Wednesday night service or a small group in another building or place. The youth had their own building where they met and had church or other activities.

Eden began to disobey and get in trouble. During this time, alcohol consumed much of her dad's life, and to add to the problem, he was always available to hand out money to her. He more or less wanted to be her friend instead of her dad and at times covered for the lies that she would tell me about where she was, who she was with, and what she was doing.

It came time for homecoming at school. Eden wanted a new dress, so her dad gave her the money to go shopping. She went to a store in our local mall with one of her friends from church to pick out this new prom dress. The next thing I know, I got a phone call from Strickland Youth Center that Eden and her friend had been arrested for shoplifting! The man who did the intake during this time at Strickland also went to church with us and his wife taught at my children's elementary school. I know now this was only the beginning. More than embarrassed, I was mad, but mostly hurt and upset, not understanding what was happening to our daughter. I truly did not want her going down the "wrong road". I did not have a clue as to why she would steal a dress that her dad had given her enough money to buy.

I would not realize until later the pride I had built up in my heart over the idea of raising the "perfect daughters"; now that world was slipping away and I had no control. Mothers, check yourself to make sure that you haven't made raising your children about making yourself look good even though the thoughts and ideas that you have and want for your children are good. It's important to want Jesus for your children because they need a Savior, not because of your own pride.

EDEN'S PERSPECTIVE

Not only did I have toxic friendships, but it was the beginning of toxic relationships with boys. I know my dad loved me, but I felt cheated by his alcohol. I was devastated that he chose alcohol over me. Having a broken relationship with my dad at such a young age, I found myself looking for a male figure who would choose me.

I now realize that not having a good marriage modeled for me nor a dad to show me what real love looks like began a long journey of looking for love and fulfillment in all the wrong people, places, and things. I started dating a boy who was involved in my church youth group. He was the drummer in the worship band at our church. My mom was totally against me dating in the first place, but I did it behind her back. This relationship stirred up a rebellion in me that I had never experienced. It says in Ephesians 6:1, "Children obey your parents in the Lord for this is right." Today, I understand this now more than ever having come through a hard road of rebellion.

Mom tried to explain to me that it wasn't
enough for her to want Jesus for me—that
I needed to want Him for myself.

One afternoon my mom was going to take my younger sister, Mary Kathryn, and me to a movie. I acted like I was sick so I could take this opportunity to sneak my boyfriend over to our house. He did not have a vehicle so one of his friends drove him to my home. Before they left, I asked my sister to cover for me and text me so I would know when they would be home. I didn't want to get caught, but that didn't work out so well.

My mom had this "feeling" she needed to turn around and come back home, leaving Mary Kathryn no time to warn me. I would soon learn that the Holy Spirit had a way of talking to my mom about her kids. Before I knew it, Mom and Mary Kathryn were walking back through the front door much sooner than I expected!

Here I was with my boyfriend and his friend in my bedroom ... not good. Seemed to me the only logical thing to do was to hide them in my closet. My heart was pounding, and I jumped into my bed, closed my eyes, and pretended like I was taking a nap. It never dawned on me that my friend's truck was parked right out in front of our house and my mom had seen it. Genius, I know. What a flawless plan.

Of course, my mom came in wondering whose truck was parked out front. She walked into my room and began questioning me. I acted like I had been asleep and didn't know what she was talking about. She wasn't falling for it. She went straight to the closet, flung open the door, and found those boys squatting on the floor. I will never forget the look of terror in their eyes. It certainly wasn't funny that day, but we did have a good laugh about it much later as we recalled the look of fear on their faces when Mom opened that closet door. My mom was so mad and put me on restriction. I got my cell phone taken away and was not allowed to go anywhere with my friends for a month. She talked with my youth pastor, and I was not allowed to hang with my boyfriend at church. Mom tried to explain to me that it wasn't enough for her to want Jesus for me—that I needed to want Him for myself. I was young and wanted to do what I wanted to do. I continued to see him without my Mom's knowledge or consent. I now wish I would have listened.

CHAPTER 3

Unexpected Death

The LORD is close to the brokenhearted and
saves those who are crushed in spirit.
—PSALMS 34:18

STEVE'S SALVATION

A few months after Eden was born, I remember sitting in church and Steve was holding her. My dad was preaching and when it came time for the altar call at the end of the service, Steve stood up, walked all the way down the center aisle with Eden in his arms, tears streaming down his face. He knelt at the altar, prayed, and gave his heart to Jesus.

After this new beginning for Steve, we went from just attending church to serving in church. We served in the children's church for a while. He later went on to teach an adult Sunday School class. I was proud and surprised at the same time because he was very introverted and had not been involved in church. After quite some time, he began to miss church here and there, stopped teaching Sunday School, and eventually quit going to church.

I believe that Steve wanted to be free and sober. For reasons we may never understand, he eventually went back to drinking and never returned to church other than occasional visits. Somewhere in this generational curse of addiction, someone has to stand up and say "Enough, it stops right here!" Break the cycle of addiction. Make a decision that it will not continue through you, that you will not pass it on to your children. Get whatever help you need.

BROKEN MARRIAGE

I had never been around alcohol much or an alcoholic, for that matter.

Honestly, I thought all alcoholics were homeless and lived under a bridge. After dating only six months, Steve and I were married on May 12th, 1989. I soon learned that Steve was what is considered a "functional alcoholic". Having lived through that time in my life, those two words together seem like an oxymoron. In my book, the words "functional" and "alcoholic" did not go together. When we dated Steve drank, but I didn't realize he had a problem and I even joined him a few times myself, but I knew this wasn't something I wanted in my life. I started thinking *this is a lot of drinking*, and even though he got drunk, I still had no thought of him being an alcoholic. As time went on and we talked of marriage, I made it known that I had to make decisions for my life and family and alcohol had to end because there was no room in my family for it. I also said, "I'm not trying to tell you what to do; it's your life, and you get to choose. But if alcohol is what you want, then I can't be a part of it." He said he would stop drinking. He did, and we were married shortly after that decision. About two months into the marriage, he came home with some flowers and alcohol on his breath one day. We had a huge argument over it, and I thought everything was fixed. A few weeks later I found out I was pregnant with Eden. To my knowledge, he was sober . . . until she was born. The week we came home from the hospital, he got drunk again. Once again, an argument, and once again, everything was fixed. He stayed sober for quite some time. It's hard to explain, but he would go through long stints of sobriety and then "fall off the wagon".

When Steve was in his 40s, the doctors diagnosed him with Hepatitis C with cirrhosis. Eden was around ten years old. The doctors explained to him that if he continued to drink, he would die. Steve stopped drinking and began an intense medical treatment that drastically improved his condition. We were able to enjoy some fun sober time. Unfortunately, the sobriety again ended. A little over a year later, he returned to alcohol. Steve refused to commit himself to rehab. He always believed he could do it on his own.

We pretty much lived separate lives during most of our marriage. I would always take the kids with me. I could not leave them there with their dad drinking. We were far from perfect. Sadly, there are no "do-overs" for parents. We made our share of mistakes. One day in marriage counseling, the therapist made this statement: "It's better for kids to come from a broken home than to be raised in one." Why didn't I listen?! I feared I could not make it on my own. Looking back, I realize I should have removed my children and myself completely from that situation. I believe safety should be found where there is abuse or substance addiction. I also struggled with my own codependency and unresolved pain from my past.

I have my reasons and some excuses, but I can't even answer all of my own questions as to why I stayed in that marriage. For most of our married life, I was a stay-at-home mom and wanted it to remain that way. I did not want my children in daycare. By no means do I want to blame only my husband for our failed marriage. We each brought enough baggage into the marriage that would have sunk the Titanic before it ever hit that iceberg!

Finally, I did get to the point where I wanted out no matter what it took, and once again, we were separated. I started working part-time as a real estate assistant while taking a few classes at the University of South Alabama with the plan of becoming a registered nurse.

All through this back-and-forth separation, we never divorced. At this point in our marriage, we had lived separated for several years. Around 2005, I hired an attorney and drew up divorce papers that Steve never signed. He did not want a divorce and seemed content with our separate lives, but for me, our marriage had been over for years. Sadly, work got the best of his sober hours but on most days he was drunk by 4:00 p.m. Eventually "drunk" consumed most of his day.

OUR LAST VISIT

Our wedding anniversary was May 12th, but we didn't celebrate that anymore. What had started out in 1989 as a joyous day was more like a day of regret eighteen years later. Looking back, I can see the mercy of the Lord that even though we didn't celebrate that day anymore, for some reason I felt drawn to go visit him on our anniversary in 2007, which was on a Saturday.

No arguments or fights—we just sat, talked, and even laughed. We had a nice visit for about an hour and a half. I had no idea when I said goodbye to him that afternoon that it would be the last time I would see him alive. I thank the Lord for this special visit.

Lindy had been living down in Florida and was in Mobile visiting. Sunday morning, she stopped by to say goodbye to Steve on her way back to Florida. On Sunday afternoon, Eden and Mary Kathryn took our boxer, Bones, over to their dad's for him to dog sit for a few days. Bones was a handful, and we needed a break. They weren't there long—a quick in-and-out visit. Little did they know this would be their last goodbye, too.

FAMILY TRAGEDY

Tuesday, May 15, 2007, started out as a normal day in the life at the Metzger home. I went to work, Eden and Mary Kathryn went to school. There was a bomb threat early that morning after they arrived at school, so they left and gave a ride to a couple of other friends. After they dropped their friends off, they called their dad to ask him if he would buy them a video game. After several phone calls with no answer, Eden called me at work to say they had tried several times to call their dad and couldn't get him on the phone. She said they were going to drive to his house to see if he was home.

"If you get there and your dad's truck is in the driveway, don't go in," I told them. "Call me, and I will come and see about him." I don't know why, but a strange feeling came over me. I felt like maybe something was wrong. I began to pray. I now know it was the Holy Spirit protecting our girls.

When the girls arrived at his house, Eden called me to say that their dad's truck was there. "We knocked and rang the doorbell, but got no answer," she said. I told them not to go into the house. She told me that they even knocked on every window and there was no answer. I repeated, "Do not go in the house. Let me come and see what's going on."

My parents, Mamaw and Papaw, lived about seven minutes away, so I told my girls to go to Mamaw and Papaw's house and wait for my call. I started feeling like something must be wrong. It wasn't like him not to answer our calls, especially if he was not out on a job with his crane inspection company.

Back at my real estate assistant job, we were having difficulties with a house closing, and it was taking a little longer than expected. Finally, I knew I had to leave and told my boss I have to go check on my husband. This day will forever be burned in my memory.

I pulled in the driveway and saw that Steve's truck was there. As I walked up to the door my mind began to race with questions. Is he passed out drunk? Getting drunk and falling had been happening often, so my thoughts were, *did he get drunk, fall, and really hurt himself this time*? As I opened the door my heart began to pound. I can't explain it, but there was an eerie silence in the house. I called out "Steve, Steve," but no answer.

It wasn't long before the EMTs came
back out and told us he was gone.

I walked into the great room in the back of the house, thinking maybe he was passed out in his recliner, but he wasn't there. I could barely breathe as I walked down the hall toward the bedroom still calling his name, "Steve, Steve." The bedroom door was open and there he was lying in bed. He was unresponsive to my calls.

I stood at the bedroom door and began to scream his name, "Steve, Steve!" No movement. I was so terrified; I could not walk over to him because I could see that his skin was a gray/ashen color as if he had passed away. I grabbed the phone and ran out of the house to the front porch.

I called 911 on the house phone and called my mom on my cell phone. I cannot remember the whole call, but the 911 operator asked, "Ma'am, is he breathing?" "I don't know. I don't think so," I said.

"Ma'am, I'm going to need you to go see if he's breathing."

I'm panicking. "I can't. I think he's dead! He's like a gray color. . . . he looks dead!" The 911 operator kept insisting. Frantically I yelled, "I think he's dead, I can't do it!"

At this point I was crying, praying, and could barely breathe as I paced back and forth on the front porch while waiting for the EMT. My parents and the ambulance arrived at the same time. The paramedics went into the bedroom to check on him. My parents and I were waiting in the living room. Everything seemed to move in slow motion. It wasn't long before the EMTs came back out and told us he was gone. I collapsed onto the sofa sobbing. My Dad just held me. They went on to say that he had been dead for a long while and it was too late for them to try and revive him.

We did not want to tell my girls over the phone, but right after the EMT had told us he was deceased, Eden called my mom's cell phone and said, "Mamaw just tell us, we can take it. Is he dead!!?"

"Yes I'm so sorry," Mamaw responded. Eden and Mary Kathryn sobbed. They then called their older two sisters, hysterically crying to tell them, "Dad is dead!"

I was so upset I didn't even think about our dog, Bones. Before I left the house, I heard him whimpering in the back bedroom. I went back there and opened the door. He was so happy to see me. He had messed all over that room, indicating he had been closed in there for a while. I let him outside, gave him some water, loaded him up, and took him home.

We all met back up at our other house where the girls and I were living. My daughter Kristin lived in Minnesota where she was attending college. We arranged for her and her boyfriend, Shawn (now her husband), to fly in the next day. When she arrived, my four girls and I closed ourselves into my bedroom, climbed into my bed, and sobbed from the bottom of our souls. Shawn waited in our living room and later told us that was the worst sound he had ever heard.

We would later discover that Steve most likely passed away Sunday night or in the early hours of Monday morning. This was the timeline: I had a visit with him Saturday afternoon, Lindy had seen him Sunday morning, and the girls had taken the dog there Sunday evening. We listened to his answering machine and there was a message that had been left on Monday morning from one of his crane clients asking where he was because he had not shown up to inspect their cranes. Although I was told that he had been dead for a couple of days, they still put Tuesday, May 15,

2007, on the death certificate because that was the date we found him. Later on that week, after some testing by the coroner, they deemed the cause of death to be hypertension related to chronic ethanol abuse. Our family was devastated. Our lives were a mess.

EDEN'S PERSPECTiVE

Losing my dad was devastating. There are no words to describe that pain—even though he was an alcoholic and I was hurt by him in so many ways because he chose alcohol over me, missing birthdays, sports events . . . and just generally was not there for me because he was drunk. It's hard to explain the pain and turmoil of having an alcoholic parent. But at this moment, none of that seemed to matter. He was my dad and I loved him so much. I could go over to his house and hang out with him, and for some reason, I knew I could go to him if I needed to—if I needed anything—but now he was gone forever.

All my hopes of one day having a sober dad were gone. All those prayers I had prayed for years now seemed useless and unanswered. I was left with the difficult question, "Where were you, God?" A question I could not answer and didn't know where to begin. So many unanswered questions, so much pain, that all led to so much anger.

CHAPTER 4

The Prodigal Leaves Home— A Life on Drugs

*He began to be in need. . . . When he came to his senses
. . . he said I will go back to my Father and say to him:
I have sinned against heaven and against you.*
LUKE 15:14-18 (AUTHOR PARAPHRASE)

GOING TO COLLEGE

After losing her dad, Eden seemed to lose her way. She did not want to return to her high school that next school year after her dad had passed away. I told her she had to graduate. She said she wanted to attend a school with a pace program for her senior year. So we enrolled her in a pace program in the fall of 2007 and she graduated at the end of that same year.

Soon after graduation, I helped her move to Birmingham, Alabama to live with Steve's dad, Papoo. We went up there and fixed up the whole upstairs of Papoo's home for Eden to have her own space. The plan was for her to attend Jefferson Community College. I was praying for a fresh start. I bought her a car so she would have a way to get around. One rule was attached to the privilege of this vehicle. The agreement was that she could have this car as long as she didn't drink, do drugs, or party. She registered for college and a got part-time job. But I soon discovered that she went up there to escape my rules and party. Sadly, it wasn't about a fresh start or college. A few months later, I drove up there one night and picked up the car that I had bought her and brought it back to our house in Mobile. It seemed she was nowhere ready to be responsible. The rebellious road was calling, and I knew the pain from losing her dad was adding to it. It wasn't long before she left her granddad's and moved back home. She was still struggling to get her life back together.

A MIDNIGHT KNOCK AT THE DOOR

After she moved back home the rebellion grew. She was in and out with friends and I knew this had to end. One night after moving back home, Eden had gone to spend the night with some friends. Late that night, I heard a knock on the door. I went downstairs, opened the front door, and a friend of Eden's was standing there literally holding her up. I let them inside and somehow, we managed to get Eden upstairs. It was pouring down rain and her clothes were soaking wet. It appeared she was very intoxicated. Eden was crying but did not seem to be able to tell us what was wrong.

The friend who had brought her to our house told me that Eden had called her to pick her up and that she did not know what was going on or if Eden had taken drugs or been drinking. We took her wet clothes off, put a nightshirt on her, and put her in my bed. As soon as we got her in bed, she was out, sound asleep. I was too afraid to let her sleep alone. I felt like I needed to watch over her. I laid hands on her and prayed all night, staying awake and watching her breathe. At times her breathing would slow down, and I would shake her. It was a long night. For me, there would be many more long nights staying awake praying, but she would not be by my side, because most of these nights I had no idea where she was, who she was with, what she was doing, or if she was even still alive.

TRIP TO MINNESOTA AFTER DEVASTATING NEWS

After this long night of worry and no sleep, we had plane tickets for the next day to go visit her sisters, Mary Kathryn and Kristin in Minnesota. Mary Kathryn was now living in Minnesota with Kristin. When I woke Eden up that morning to get ready, she still seemed quite hungover, but we had survived the night through the grace of God. We got up and got ready. I had to keep her on task. At that moment I was determined we were going to Minnesota; the tickets cost too much money, they couldn't be exchanged, and they were non-refundable.

Now that we made it through the night, I was upset with her. I was tired and fed up with the way alcohol and drugs were ruining our lives. It's like you get so angry because it's easier than dealing with the pain and hurt because you absolutely don't know what to do, you have no control, and you're just trying to survive and praying your child survives. On one hand, you're wondering when or if it's ever going to end, and on the other hand, you're filled with fear of the thought of how it might end.

I said, "Why are you doing this Eden? What is going on?" She sat down on the sofa and began to sob. When I asked her what was wrong, she could barely speak. Desperation has a sound—the sound of my daughter sobbing while I held her in my arms as she explained to me that she had been raped. I felt like something inside of me died; the thought of that happening to one of my children was devastating. Like being kicked in the gut. I couldn't even imagine how she felt. I immediately called our attorney only to hear him say it would be her word against theirs and that they would say she traded sex for drugs. I argued back because I just couldn't accept this answer. This was a horrific traumatic offense against my daughter! As much as I hated it, I knew that what he was saying could possibly be true, but I wanted justice for my daughter! I thought maybe I could take her to the hospital, but she said it had happened last week. Rape is rape even if you are addicted to drugs. You're still a person and your life matters. No one should ever have to go through the traumatic experience of rape!

At this point, the cost of the airline tickets and the anger I felt toward her rebellion no longer mattered. My heart was broken for her. I told her that we didn't have to go on the trip. I don't know if it was the residual effects from her hangover talking, but she said she wanted to go.

I tried to explain to her that the airline's policy does not allow people "under the influence" to get on the plane. So I instructed her that when we arrived at the airport to hold on to my arm, walk with me and don't say a word. I told her that if they asked any questions to just be quiet and that I would handle it. I wasn't sure if we would be able to get on the plane. We just wanted to get to Minnesota. We made it on the first plane and landed at our first stop.

I began to realize and had to admit to myself

that Eden was not just rebellious, but that she

had a real problem with drugs and alcohol.

I had to go to the bathroom, so I sat Eden out in the waiting area and said to her "Do not move, I'll be right back." When I got back, of course she was gone. I thought *Dear Lord, help me.* At about that time, these sliding doors came open to a closed-off room for smokers. I have no idea how she could have gotten herself there, but I looked up and there she was sitting up in a chair asleep with a cigarette in her hand. I went in, took her by the hand, and said, "Come on ,we need to get to our next gate."

Looking back at the insanity of my life, I often wonder why I did the things I did. It feels like I was just in survival mode. When I read my own book, I can't believe this was my life.

Somehow, we were able to board the next plane and arrived safely in Minnesota. All I can say is God's grace follows me.

There are no words to describe the heartache, pain, and destruction that drugs and drug addiction will bring to your life and family. It affects every single part of your life! I began to realize and had to admit to myself that Eden was not just rebellious, but that she had a real problem with drugs and alcohol.

RULE OF THE HOUSE

One of the worst things you could ever hear as a parent is that your child is addicted to drugs. Shortly after we returned from Minnesota, Eden left our home to go live with two of her friends who were living with their dad and didn't have the "rules" that we had at our house. Once again, she was lured back to drugs by the power of addiction. I begged Eden to stay and get help. Desperation has a sound. The sound of that front door slamming with your daughter refusing help. I had prayed and prayed for Eden to come back to the Lord, always imagining it to be like the Prodigal Son story, or in my case, the "Prodigal Daughter". In my mind I would imagine that she would be in a life of rebellion, slopping with the pigs when suddenly she would remember the life she had back home. The light bulb would come on, she would come back to her senses and return home.

Luke 15:17 says of the prodigal son, "When he came to his senses". This implies the prodigal son was not in his right mind.

When we are in rebellion against the Lord, we just aren't in our right minds or we wouldn't be "mud ridin'" with the pigs!

I had imagined that I would hear this knock at the door, because at this point, she no longer had a key to our house.

This too broke my heart—I really struggled with it. I had a rule, "You can't live in our house and do drugs." Sadly, Eden chose drugs and made a decision to leave our house. This was a very difficult time for Eden and the enemy was relentlessly pursuing her to destroy her life. Jesus was pursuing her to give her life.

During this time, Eden's version was a little different. She told her friends, "Mama kicked me out." Maybe for her that sounded better, or somehow made her feel better. Nevertheless, the entire situation was very upsetting for both of us. As her mom, I had given my whole life to love, nurture, and protect her, so how could I be in this place where she could no longer live in our house?

One morning as I lay in bed, sobbing and crying out to the Lord about all of this, I said, "God am I doing the right thing? Help me, God. You know I have messed up and made plenty of bad decisions in my life and You would never lock me out of Your house."

I sensed the Holy Spirit saying, "Rebellion separates you from the Father, and prevents you from being in His house and living in His favor and in His presence, although His love remains the same. It's like that with our own kids. Their rebellion in a sense has locked them out of the house, although your love for them remains the same. Lori, you haven't locked them out. They are choosing it." I realized in that moment that she was choosing rebellion over the blessing.

The Holy Spirit was saying, "Just like when you choose to be in rebellion against me, it keeps you from receiving the Father's blessings. It's your own decisions that lock you out." The bottom line to that entire situation was that it was up to Eden; it was her choice. I heard this quote that gave me a good perspective: "The only people who get upset about you setting boundaries are the ones who were benefiting from you NOT having any."[2]

I don't claim to have all the answers or the perfect solution or even to know what boundaries need to be set when you have a child who is addicted to drugs. I have lived through it and have learned from it. We do need to be careful not to co-sign with the addiction or sin. I do know this—never stop loving, never stop praying, and never give up. Jesus is our only HOPE!

WAITING ON THE PRODIGAL'S RETURN

The Prodigal Son story in Luke 15 tells us that sometime after the son left, he "began to be in need" and it was then that "he came to his senses." It says this happened after he had spent everything. Notice in this story the Father did not run after the son and did not have access to a Western Union to continue funneling money to him. Nowadays, God can't even work in our kids' lives because us parents are too busy intervening. If we don't watch it, we will support them all the way to their death. It has been said this way: "When the pain of remaining the same becomes greater than the pain of change, that's when you will change." I understand that it is very difficult to know what to do when all of this is happening. There's no manual on how to parent rebellious teenagers, especially not ones dealing with addiction. Many times, it is out of our need and out of our desperation that we begin to seek God. I know

---

2   Brian Weiner, "The Only People Who Get Upset about You Setting Boundaries Are Those Who Are Benefitting from You Having None," BrianWeiner.com, n.d., https://brianweiner.com/the-only-people-who-get-upset-about-you-setting-boundaries-are-those-who-are-benefitting-from-you-having-none/.

from first-hand experience that it is very hard to allow your kids to become desperate so they will seek the Lord. It can be downright scary, especially when we are looking at them and not Him.

Yes, I did imagine that our story would be similar to the Prodigal Son story. I would open the door, and she would be standing there, tears streaming down her cheeks, saying "Mom, I'm sorry, can I come home? I need Jesus!" She would come inside, get cleaned up, and we would go to a restaurant and eat, because unlike the prodigal son's dad, I didn't have a fatty calf. Nor did I have any servants to kill the fatty calf and cook it.

I imagined that after our delicious dinner, we would spend the rest of the night sitting around talking about Jesus. The reality is this did not happen. The more I prayed the worse it got.

Have you heard, "God will never give you more than you can bear?"

It is a lie and it's not in the Bible! Often this verse in Corinthians is misquoted. What it says is this: God will not let you be tempted beyond what you can bear (1 Corinthians 10:13, author paraphrased) But this I know: He will give you more than you can take and allow more to be put on you than you can bear, so that you realize "apart from me you can do nothing!" (John 15:5) I was desperate for God to intervene.

Most of the time I didn't know where Eden was staying. She went from boyfriend to boyfriend and every once in a while, she would come by the house for a short visit.

EDEN'S PERSPECTIVE

I felt like I had lost my closest friend—my sister Kristin—in fall of 2006, when she left to attend college in Minnesota. Her leaving was really hard on me. We spent a lot of time together hanging out with our friends from church, who were mostly her age. Not long after she left for college, I started hanging with the wrong group of people. It was then that I began to lose interest in church and living my life for Jesus. In May 2007, only nine months after my sister left for college, my Dad passed away. At the young age of seventeen, my life seemed to go from bad to worse and began to really spiral. I was so mad at God and felt justified. After all, wasn't He responsible for my Dad's death? I had prayed all my life for him to stop drinking! It was now time for me to return to school even though my life was in total turmoil. What should have been a time of celebrating my senior year became a year of overwhelming pain and sorrow.

I did not want to go back to school, but my Mom said quitting was not an option. In the fall of 2007, rather than returning to the high school that I had attended since my freshman year, I enrolled in a pace program and graduated early.

Soon after I graduated, I moved up to Birmingham with my Papoo. My mom and I had fixed up the upstairs of his house as "my space". The plan was for me to attend Jefferson State Community College, but I found friends to drink and get high with instead of going to school. When she gave me the car, the rule was that there would be no drinking, drugging, or partying, and if I did I would lose the privilege of the vehicle. Now that I had dropped out of college with no way to get around in Birmingham, I moved back home. I would go off with friends, hang out, do drugs, and go back home. This went on for a while and I eventually left home. I was planning on moving out again, but this time with two of my friends.

One night before I moved out, I went to spend the night with some of my other friends who were having a party at their parents' house. We ran out of cocaine, so I called my dealer to see if he would "front" me some drugs, but he was out of town. "Front" me some drugs means you get drugs now and pay for them later. He said his brother had some that he would "front" me. So I called him and he agreed. We drove to Prichard, a town on the outskirts of Mobile where there is a ton of drug activity and violence. My friends stayed in the car to wait for me while I went inside the house to get the drugs.

The drug dealer met me at the door, we walked through the living room where there were two older women sitting on the couch just watching TV. He then led me to the back bedroom where his cousin was waiting with the drugs. I snorted a line of cocaine but had no idea what was about to happen to me. These same men sexually assaulted and raped me. It was a night from hell, I couldn't believe this was happening. I was terrified and didn't know if I was going to get out alive! All I can remember is trying to get them off of me and yelling over and over, "Stop!" I thought, *where are those two women that I saw when I walked into the house? Didn't they hear my screams?* We were in the room right next to where they were sitting!

When I finally made it out of that house and got back to the car, I told my friends what had happened. Sadly, they offered no help, addiction and partying outweighed my own self-worth. As crazy as this sounds, we just went back to the party waiting for us at their house. I acted like nothing had happened but inside, I was a wreck. This was the devastating reality of my life as an addict. The condition of my life was a mess: no self-love, no self-worth. I was at the bottom with no hope. That night, I did so many drugs trying to numb myself. The truth is you can't do enough drugs to forget the trauma of being sexually assaulted. I stayed with my friends that night and didn't speak of this again until about a week later when I told my mom.

It was easier to decide I didn't believe in God than to face the fact that He is real.

The next day I called my "drug dealer", the one that had sent me over there to get the drugs from his brother. I told him what happened. To my surprise, he asked me why I didn't call the police. I wished I could have called the police but the sad truth is that I was there to get drugs and too messed up to even give a description of the house where it took place or even what the two men looked like. Not only that, I feared the consequences of trying to have them arrested. It is an understood thing in the drug world that you don't call the police. Even though I was there to get drugs, I would never see justice for being raped.

I didn't care about my life or anything else for that matter. I was so devastated over losing my dad and going through a traumatic rape that I just wanted to be numb all of the time. By now I was smoking weed almost every single day and taking Xanax as often as I could. My mom had made it clear that I could either live at home and stop doing drugs or I could move out. She wanted to help me and offered to take me to rehab, but at this time I just wanted to do drugs and didn't want her help or her telling me what to do. I made arrangements to move into my friend's house where she and her sister lived with their dad. My partying only escalated from there. No rules, no boundaries, free to do what I wanted to do, but what I didn't consider is that this so-called "freedom" came with a price. I was indeed free to do whatever I wanted, but not free from the consequences.

I was indeed free to do whatever I wanted,

but not free from the consequences.

I began to live a promiscuous lifestyle. I had no self-love or worth. Not long after I moved in with my friends, I started dating their brother. I did not know then that he was taking pain pills regularly. Soon after I began dating him, I was prescribed pain meds. This prescription opened the door for my addiction to pain pills, along with the pills my boyfriend was providing. Unfortunately, addiction ran so heavy in my dad's family—he, his mom, and his siblings—had all passed away from drug and alcohol addiction. So, when I took this prescribed pain medication, I was immediately hooked.

I left the house where I was living with my boyfriend's sisters and moved in with him. We spent most of our time living out our addiction to pain pills. He didn't believe in God, so I decided I wasn't going to either. I claimed to be an atheist, but I was really just so broken and mad at God that he had taken my Dad. I had prayed and prayed for years that my Dad would stop drinking. I was an angry, hurt girl whose life was spiraling out of control. It was easier to decide I didn't believe in God than to face the fact that He is real. Because if He's real, that meant first of all I would have to deal with the way I was living my life in rebellion against God, and I was nowhere near ready for that—I would have had to admit that it was Dad's own choices that killed him and not God—and I wasn't ready to deal with that either.

CHAPTER 5

Leave the Past Behind

Forget the former things; do not dwell on the past. See, I am doing a new thing! Now it springs up; do you not perceive it? I am making a way in the wilderness and streams in the wasteland.
—Isaiah 43:18-19

GOING TO REHAB

The fear of Eden dying would often grip my soul. Eden had been living with a new boyfriend who kept her supplied with pills and alcohol. Then came the day in 2010 I had been praying and waiting for. Eden came home and told us she wanted to get sober. She had made arrangements for herself to go to the Home of Grace, a rehab center in Mobile, Alabama. All the women there call it "HOG", short for Home of Grace. I had heard good things about Home of Grace. Eden came to our house and asked me to take her. I said sure, but I did not know how to get there and did not have GPS. Before she came to our house, she had called the intake person to make arrangements to get accepted into their program, and they gave her directions to the facility. There was one big problem when she got to our house: she was so messed up on drugs that she could barely walk. I think she must have wanted one last hoorah before going to rehab, where she would have to give it all up. It was storming that day, but I was so desperate for her to get sober, I didn't care if we had to take a boat! For me, it wasn't just a matter of her getting sober, but finding her way back to freedom, to Jesus, life, and self-love.

Mary Kathryn, her younger sister, decided to ride with us and help me get her there. When we got Eden into our truck, it was raining so hard that I could barely see in front of me. Eden was so high that she could not remember the directions, only the general vicinity. So needless to say, we got lost several times. Eden suggested that we just go back home, and I said, "No way." I knew this was life or death and turning back was not an option. Need I say, heated conversations were an understatement; we needed some Jesus up in that truck. We were screaming and yelling at each other, when all of a sudden, through the pouring down rain, we looked up and there was a sign for Home of Grace on Hallelujah Lane. We all just started laughing because we thought it was so funny that the street was called Hallelujah Lane. We needed to raise a hallelujah up in that truck after all that fussing we had been doing. I knew it was only the Grace of God that got us there. Somehow, we got her out of the truck and inside the "HOG".

Everyone was so kind and helpful. This was nothing new for them. They took Eden in and had someone watch over her night and day during this time of detoxing. She was assigned a counselor who was a great help to her during her time at the Home of Grace.

Our family visited her every week. We brought her gifts and snacks that were allowed according to the guidelines on the list that we were given when we dropped her off. Eden did well at the "HOG". During these few months, it was such a relief to see the light and life come back into her beautiful brown eyes!

What we didn't know was that her sobriety would be short-lived. As we were nearing the end of her ninety days, I heard the news that she was still in contact with the "drug" boyfriend she had been living with before she came to rehab. This was devastating to me. We all knew she would be trading her new life of sobriety if she went back with him, but no matter what we said, she was not hearing it. We prayed but it did not change her heart. Nevertheless, graduation day came and we were so excited that Eden had stayed and finished the ninety-day rehab program and now had the tools to live life sober. Sadly, it was just that—ninety days. Home of Grace has an extended program where the women can stay longer, and they will work with you and help you stay true to your sobriety. After graduating from Home of Grace, sobriety ended for Eden that day, but not forever. God was not done writing her story. Instead of coming home with us to live sober, she went back to her boyfriend and a life of drugs. I heard this saying one time and sadly, it's true: sin will take you further than you ever wanted to go, cost you more than you ever wanted to pay, and keep you longer than you ever wanted to stay.

YOUR EYES ARE THE WINDOW OF YOUR SOUL

There is no pain like realizing your beautiful little girl has no self-love or self-worth. How did this happen? How did we get here? Where did we go wrong? I did not know what to do. Somedays I didn't even know if I could keep on going. "Jesus, just help me breathe!"

If your soul is dark, then your eyes will transmit darkness. If light is in your soul, then your eyes will transmit light.

It broke my heart into a million pieces to see the deep, dark sadness that came from Eden's eyes, an emptiness like I had never seen before. It was as if there was no life in her.

"The eye is the lamp of the body. If your eyes are healthy, your whole body will be full of light. But if your eyes are unhealthy, your whole body will be full of darkness. If then the light within you is darkness, how great is that darkness!" (Matthew 6:22-23)

It is true—the eyes are the windows of your soul. As if to say, what's in your soul is transmitted through your eyes. If your soul is dark, then your eyes will transmit darkness. If light is in your soul, then your eyes will transmit light. I understood and witnessed this as I looked into my own daughter's big brown eyes.

I knew she needed the light of Jesus now more than ever!!

EDEN'S PERSPECTIVE

I was living a life of total destruction. I honestly didn't care if I lived or died. Many times, I wished I wouldn't even wake up. My relationship with my last boyfriend had ended, but my addiction to pain pills hadn't. My life was out of control. I was exhausted from "hustling" day and night just to get my next high, not stopping at anything—at this point, even selling or trading my body for drugs. It seemed to me the only way to survive because sobriety seemed unreachable, and withdrawal was not an option. An addict will go to great lengths to avoid withdrawals at almost any cost. Withdrawing "cold turkey" from pain pills is horrible. Every inch of your body hurts. You are in excruciating pain, at times vomiting while profusely sweating and somehow shaking with chills. I longed to be free but did not know how. I felt hopeless.

My oldest sister, Lindy, had been addicted to drugs for a long time and I began to hang out with her a lot during this time. I started dating one of her friends who was also taking pain meds. Every decision I made involved drugs and how I was going to get more, so moving in with him seemed like the best decision at this time. This relationship enabled my drug addiction and drinking even more because he actually had an ongoing prescription for his pain meds. After about a year into this relationship, I began to want to go back home but of course that meant I would have to get off of drugs and face withdrawals. I understand now that my mom had to have boundaries, so her rule remained that I couldn't live at home and do drugs. My family had pleaded with me on several occasions to go to rehab. This would usually tick me off and I always said, "No."

In May of 2010, I decided on my own that I was going to go to rehab so that I could prove to everyone that I could quit whenever I wanted to, and furthermore, that I could be sober if I wanted to. I called Home of Grace, a rehab facility in Mobile, and then called and asked my mom if she would take me.

I entered into a ninety-day program at the Home of Grace. Even though I went there just to "prove" that I could do it, it was a great rehab center and it provided me with all the tools that I needed in order to get sober and stay sober. The only problem? I wasn't actually ready to stay sober, but I didn't realize it at the time.

During my stay at Home of Grace, I had kept in contact with that boyfriend that I had left to come to rehab. If you know anything at all about recovery, then you know that you have to let go of ALL old people, places, and things. The saying in rehab is, "Change your playmates and your playgrounds." I would soon find out that there's a good reason for this rule. I had been out of rehab for only a few weeks and trying to stay sober for my graduation from Home of Grace. I was struggling. I did manage to make it through graduation but immediately went back to my old boyfriend and my old ways—a life of pills and alcohol.

CHAPTER 6

Right Back at It . . . and More

*Jesus said, "The thief comes only to steal and kill
and destroy; I have come that they might have life,
and that they might have it more abundantly."*
—JOHN 10:10

JESUS IS CALLING, BUT WHAT
WILL OUR ANSWER BE?

As I was thinking about Jesus calling us, it reminded me of the story of Bartimaeus in the Bible. In Mark 10 we read about a blind man, Bartimaeus, who was sitting on the side of the road begging when one day Jesus passed by. He began to shout to Jesus,

"Son of David have mercy on me!" It says when Jesus called him to come over to him . . . he threw off his cloak and jumped to his feet.

Many times in life, we find ourselves in a position where we are begging God to change our situation. When Bartimaeus cried out, everyone told him to be quiet but he "cried out all the more." The Greek here equates this "crying out" to a woman in labor. Now that's some serious crying out. When I was in labor with my second daughter, the delivery doctor had a black eye and I told him if he pushed on my stomach one more time I was going to kick him and black his other eye! Jesus is still working on me.

Bartimaeus wasn't about to let anyone keep him from his miracle. On this day, he went from begging to expecting. He jumped up and threw down his beggar's robe, expecting Jesus to do something. Too often, we don't have enough faith to let go of the past and believe God for the new thing He wants to do in our lives. We want to hold onto that old thing just in case this new thing doesn't work out. Not Bartimaeus! He let go and left that beggar's robe, believing God for his healing. Going back wasn't an option. He threw off the old robe to get the new one. Isaiah 61:10 (author paraphrase) says, "He has clothed me in a robe of His righteousness." This is available for each and every one of us. We prayed and prayed that Eden would let go of the old and believe God for something new and better. Eden may not have been physically blind, but she was blind to the hope right in front of her.

She was not ready to let go of the past, or maybe she just didn't know how. She went right back to drugs. The only thing about getting sober and then relapsing is that most of the time, you do more drugs—new drugs. That's why you see a lot of overdoses right after relapse. For now, we would keep praying and believing for her. We can never stop praying and interceding for our family. As long as there is life and breath, there is hope.

EDEN'S PERSPECTIVE

I had determined that I wasn't willing to go back to selling my body for money or drugs. Since I didn't have any money, I was going to have to figure something out. Living a life in addiction is a constant "hustle". It wasn't long before the boyfriend situation wasn't working, and I left. All I wanted to do was get high and now I was going to have to find a way to make that happen. My older sister, Lindy, had started using meth. Lindy had been hustling and in the drug scene a lot longer than me and I knew that if I went wherever she went, I would be able to do just that—get high— even if it was with a different drug than I had been using. When I was living life in addiction, I just didn't care about anything but getting high. I began a journey of rapid destruction with my sister, living a life on crystal meth.

There are a lot of ways to do meth. I started out by smoking it, but I wasn't getting high. I was then introduced to snorting it, and that changed everything. I would eventually shoot it up intravenously. My number one goal after that was just to stay high and do whatever I had to do in order to make that happen.

We knew the shadows were demons.

Lindy and I moved in with an older man who had been one of our main sources for pills and money. One night, we called someone to "Front us some pills but didn't have a way to get to him. So, we decided to walk, which we often did. It was dark but we didn't care. Life in addiction just brings you to a place where you just don't care. Your body craves the drug, and your mind is consumed by the thoughts of getting more or when you will get more before your body goes into withdrawal. You don't care about yourself or anyone else. You will go to drastic lengths to get drugs. Safety, good reasoning, and sense are no part of the drive of addiction.

We walked several miles in the dark that night to get to this gas station in order to get our drugs. Soon after we started walking, we began to hear footsteps behind us. We were the only ones on the street so how was it we were hearing footsteps? We looked back and saw a dark shadow. In the meth world, we call them "shadow people," which are basically demonic beings said to be delusions from lack of sleep. We were afraid but we didn't let that stop us or make us turn back from what we were doing. We kept walking because we needed the drugs. We knew the shadows were demons. The drug world is a dark demonic place. At times we could literally feel the darkness. The Bible talks about drugs, using the word *pharmakeia*, referring to sorcery or magic (See Revelations 9:21, Revelations 18:23, and Galatians 5:19-21).

Galatians 5:17 says, "For the flesh desires what is contrary to the Spirit, and the Spirit what is contrary to the flesh. They are in conflict with each other, so that you are not to do whatever you want." It goes on to say in Ephesians 6:12, "For our struggle is not against flesh and blood, but against the rulers, against the authorities, against the powers of this dark world and against the spiritual forces of evil in the heavenly realms." This refers to the "enemy of my soul" that my Mom spoke of in chapter two.

Lindy began to date a guy named Greg P. He soon became her boyfriend and our meth cook. We spent every day stealing whatever we could in order to get the supplies we needed to cook dope. Day in and day out, that was our routine. We lived from one "grunge" motel to the next cooking dope in order to stay high. At one point we got to live in a trailer, but it was infested with mice and had no electricity or hot running water. This is how drugs warp your mind; we were not at all afraid of the mice. I slept on the couch and could literally hear them running around behind the couch. We would be so high that we would take flashlights and look for them. I don't even know that girl, because, in my right mind, I'm terrified of mice.

After our short stay in that trailer, we left to stay in another— what we called "drug motels". These were run-down motels that were overrun with drug activity. We only added to it.

Then everything changed for me. Around this same time, in November 2010, I met a man named Donnie. At the time, I thought he was twenty-eight years old, but later I was shocked to find out he was thirty-nine. I was only twenty at the time. This age difference didn't stop us. He was hilarious, good-looking, and charming, and we shared a similar sense of humor, but our addiction was the driving force in the relationship. Getting high was the common goal of every day and figuring out what we needed to do to make that happen. What I didn't know at the time but would soon find out was that he was a "high-ranking" member in a dangerous gang.

He told us later that he was there at this hotel on orders given by his superiors in the gang to come and see what we were about and what we were doing (referring to me and my sister, Lindy). From this point on, it was the four of us together all the time—my sister Lindy, her boyfriend Greg P., who was in a different gang, and me and my new boyfriend, Donnie.

There was a couple who would come almost every day from Dauphin Island, Alabama, to our hotel room in Mobile, Alabama, which is approximately a thirty-five-mile drive—just to get high and buy drugs.

The four of us came up with the idea that instead of this couple coming to meet us in a hotel room, we should all go live with them in the house they were renting on Dauphin Island. So, we all sat down together and convinced this couple that it would be good for all four of us to move in with them so that we would have a private place to make and do all the drugs we wanted without getting caught. When you're an addict all you think about is yourself and your next fix. So, we moved into the couple's house on Dauphin Island with them and their kids. After we moved in, we had no regard for them or the fact that this was their home. Not long after we were there, the mother left with their kids and moved back to Georgia because this was no place for kids. The dad stayed. We didn't have a car, so we just took over his car after we had already taken over his house. He was so desperate for a "fix" that he sold his car for a gram of meth, which during this time was about $100. A gram of meth would only last about a day. How quickly the enemy will rob you of everything if you allow him to take a foothold in your life. Remember, he comes to steal, kill, and destroy.

We lived here at Dauphin Island for about two months when we were finally told that we had to leave because the guy's wife and kids were coming back. Donnie and I had broken up just a day or two before because we had been arguing so frequently, and he left. Then Greg P. and Lindy decided to pack up and leave. They didn't want me to come with them. Greg P. shot me up with drugs one more time before they left and now, I would be stuck there with no drugs, no way to get back to Mobile, and nowhere to go.

I knew I was always welcome back home with my mom if and when I was ready to be drug-free, or at the least ready to get help. I should've done just that; I should have called my mom and gone home, but I didn't.

There was a battle within. I wanted to be ready to be drug-free, but my addiction ruled my life at that time. I was so far into my addiction that I thought I would never be sober. In fact, I was so depressed that every single day I literally prayed for God to kill me because I was so tired of living this way. I saw no hope in my circumstances. I never want anyone to feel this depth of hopelessness.

I cried nearly all night after Lindy and Greg P. left me. I finally ended up falling asleep because I had no more drugs. Meth is a drug that keeps you awake night and day. When you run out, the effects wear off, and you usually sleep for days.

The next morning, my mom and Lindy showed up out of nowhere to get me. Lindy had called my mom at 4:00 a.m., "Come get me—I'm with some people; they have guns and I think they're planning to kill me." Mom said she was jolted out of a dead sleep with that phone call. Lindy was hysterical and trying to explain to Mom where she was so she could come pick her up. She ran from the place she was at to a nearby Wal-Mart and told Mom to come there to get her. Mom said before she left the house, she woke her parents up in a panic and told them what was going on. She gave both of them a gun and told them not to open the door for anyone, and if anyone broke in, to shoot them. Her reasoning was that a lot of our "drug friends" knew where our house was, and she didn't know if they would come there looking for us. She didn't want to leave her parents sleeping and defenseless. Looking back, it is so sad to see what we put my mom and grandparents through. After Mom picked Lindy up, she convinced her that they needed to get to Dauphin Island and get me because my life was in danger, too. They came to Dauphin Island and picked me up. We started driving back to Mobile and as Lindy began to explain this story, I realized she was "sketching out". It's a phrase we use when someone is so badly strung out on meth that they're somewhere between psychosis and paranoia. Some of the story may be real, but most of the time it's not. Mom still believed it was real and wanted us to come with her. I was already mad at Lindy for leaving me in Dauphin Island the day before, so I said to Mom, "Take me back because Lindy is just being paranoid and sketching out." Mom begged me to come home, but I was getting so aggravated I just kept saying, "just pull over and I'll walk back," but she finally turned around and took me back to the house where she picked me up, even though everything in her was against it. The truth is you can't make another person change.

When I got back, I called Donnie and begged him to come back and get me. He showed up within the hour—a good example of the cycle of toxic relationships. We both went to live in a shed on his grandmother's property. A shed with no heat in the middle of winter. Drugs and the drive to have them will cause you to do things you never ever thought you would. The drug world is an unpredictable and dangerous place but when you're in full-blown addiction, you don't consider any of that; your only goal is to get high no matter what.

CHAPTER 7

Mom's Idols or I-Dolls

"You shall have no other gods before me."
—Exodus 20:3

SUPER MOM

I was facing some of the darkest days of my life when God began to deal with me. What was going on with my children and what I thought I needed to do to save them made me so fear-focused and overwhelmed that I was missing what God was trying to show me about myself.

I would lay in bed, wondering and asking myself, "How did we get here? How did this happen?" When my girls were younger, I had been room mom, basketball mom, dance mom, taekwondo mom, swim mom, softball mom, cheerleader mom, field trip mom, concession mom, spring break mom, piano mom, youth group mom, praying mom. I mean, I got this—I was "SUPERWOMAN," aka SUPERMOM"!!

Looking back, I realize we really spoiled our kids. As parents, we sort of had that mentality to give to our kids the things we didn't have—not that we had bad childhoods—we just wanted our kids to have more. Now I'm faced with the realization that more is not always better; less with more responsibility would have been much better for them. We gave them plenty of love, but it seems that wasn't enough.

Now I was facing the darkest days of my life. I had experienced a lot of tragedy in my own past, but when you touch one of my kids, you have touched my very heart. I turned into Mama Bear if you dared to mess with one of my cubs. I do believe as parents we are to protect our children, but there is a godly way of doing it. Sometimes as moms, we seem to take it over the top. Let's try to stop, drop, and pray instead.

TEARING DOWN IDOLS

This dark time in my life was like a lunar eclipse. According to Google Dictionary, a lunar eclipse is when the Earth gets in between the sun and the moon and blocks out the light.[3]

It's the same with us spiritually: when we allow earthly things, no matter who or what that is, to get in between us and the Son—Jesus—then the light will be blocked out. I seemed to be in total darkness. I had no light because my focus was on my children and

---

3 "Lunar eclipse," Google Dictionary, September 9, 2023, https://www.weather.gov/.

their problems and how I was going to solve those problems and save them. I could not fix this on my own, I needed to focus on the only one who could. I needed Jesus to light my path, show me the way, and give me the strength that I needed. This was way out of my control, way bigger than me, but not bigger than the power of Jesus. This reminds me of when you're going on a trip and you're sitting on the airplane getting all those safety instructions and the flight attendant says, "Be sure to put on your own oxygen mask first before assisting others." If I didn't focus on Jesus, my source of oxygen, then I would run out long before I could help my kids.

When the object through which you seek satisfaction,

fulfillment, or joy is in anything other than Jesus

Christ, it is an idol, and it will always fall short.

I allowed my problems to interfere with my view of Jesus. Jesus reminds me time and time again, speaking to my heart, "Lori stop focusing on the problem and start focusing on the problem solver—Jesus."

Even though I could not see Jesus at this time, He was there getting me through every day. Blind Bartimaeus, whom we already spoke about, couldn't see Jesus, but Jesus saw him as he was begging for help, He stopped and healed him. Genesis 16 tells us that He's the God who sees (El Roi). In Deuteronomy 3:16, God promises that He will never leave us nor forsake us. This is a promise that was not based on how I felt or what I could or couldn't see, and I held onto it!!

During this time, God began to strip off the blinders and show me myself. The only way to let the light in so that I could see the truth of my situation was to take the blinders off. I was wrong all these years that I thought I was "Super Mom". I had read the Bible for years, but it seems as you go through different situations in your life that the Holy Spirit will somehow make certain truths stand out. Right there in the Ten Commandments: "You shall have no other god besides me." (Exodus 20:2), I began to ponder what this looks like in this day and time and in my life. Modern-day idols. I was blinded to the fact that as Christians, we could actually have idols.

I sensed God saying, "Lori, you have made your children your idol. You have put them in the place that belongs only to me. You have tried to make them your source of happiness, your source of fulfillment, and only I can do that in your life."

Idols are spelled I-d-o-l-s, but for me, it was "I-d-o-l-l-s"—I had let my precious daughters become my "I-dolls", my real-life "doll babies". I have always thought of idols as a bad thing. Little ugly statues like a fat Buddha or a golden calf. What's more, I thought idol worship ended back in biblical times. We seem to get this idea as Christians that as long as we're not drinking, smoking, cussing, having immoral sex, or doing drugs, then we're good.

An idol, as I came to realize, is not necessarily a bad thing. Idols can be good things and still be wrong. Spouse, job, fitness, finance, food, church attendance—none of these are bad unless we put them in the place that belongs only to Jesus. My children were good things—blessings in my life—but I had made them into my idols. I had given them first place in my life. When the object through which you seek satisfaction, fulfillment, or joy is in anything other than Jesus Christ, it is an idol, and it will always fall short. It will NEVER satisfy!

Knowing all of this still did not make it easy for me to change. I began to pray about what to do. I knew I could not continue like I was living; I could not make it unless I changed. I felt I was on the verge of a nervous breakdown. I went to bed every night in tears, so heartbroken. Many times, I could not even pray. I could only say, "Jesus, Jesus, Jesus." The name above every name, the only one who could use my idols to bring my focus and my life back to Him.

ADVICE FROM DAD

My parents, Jim and Angela Allison, came to know Jesus in their thirties. They have been rock-solid examples of Christ in our lives. So, when Eden began to dabble with drugs, my Dad told her, "There are three ends to addiction: sobriety, prison, or death, and you have to choose." Now here I was faced with a drug-addicted daughter, and my parents stood steadfast beside me, interceding in prayer on behalf of Eden, constantly reassuring me to trust God because He is in control. My Dad would say to just love her, don't preach to her, and let the Holy Spirit do His job. Reminds me of the saying that tells us to preach the Gospel always and only use words when necessary. In other words, just live it! This was hard; if you're like me, I was always trying to tell them what to do, but they were no longer little kids.

I have been blessed with great parents who showed me the way to Jesus. My Dad was a pastor for over fifty years—he preached it and lived it. My Mom always had our house open and ready to help anyone—the hands and feet of Jesus. I can't even name the number of people whom my parents counseled and took in to stay, not to mention those fed at our table. Not bragging here, just honoring my parents and paying tribute to their love for the Lord. I am by no means saying they were perfect, there is no such a thing, but I am very thankful for them. My girls grew up very close to them. Actually, it was almost like another set of parents, except definitely a little more spoiling. My parents moved in with me shortly after my husband, Steve, passed away. My parents were a big help to me when I began to have trouble with my girls. My Dad was a very calm, levelheaded man who fully trusted in the Lord. I saw him live this daily, but it became real for me in 1979 when we were in the worst hurricane any of us had ever been through—Hurricane Frederic. It was a category four as it made landfall late at night in Mobile, AL. Most of my family were together in a tiny wooden house on a pecan orchard. Huge trees were being completely uprooted and falling everywhere; the whole house was shaking. We were all gathered by candlelight in the living room late that night listening to every terrifying news report on our battery-operated radio because by then, we had lost all power. In the middle of all of this, my Dad stood up, prayed, and said, "Goodnight, love you all, I'm going to bed." So afraid, we said, how can you go to bed?! He calmly replied, "God is in control; our life is in His hands. If we live, I'll see you all in the morning; if we die, I'll see you all in heaven." He had given it to the Lord and that was that.

My Mom, on the other hand, put her trust in the Lord, but was not going to fold her hands while she prayed but rather wring them while she prayed—but I assure you—she was praying.

One day my dad was trying to help me with some of the difficulties of raising kids. He said, "Lori, it's like this when each child is born—you have one hundred pennies. In other words, you have all the control. As they grow up slowly but surely, over the course of time, they start to take the pennies one by one and express their independence, making their own decisions and their own choices. Then one day, as they grow, you wake up and realize that you no longer have any control, no matter how hard you try, because they now have all the pennies."

A promise I have held onto says, "Train up a child in the way he should go: and when he is old, he will not depart from it" (Proverbs 22:6, KJV). This is a promise from God.

My Dad also said, "Raise them the best you can and leave it to the Lord. Don't take credit when they turn out good and don't take blame when they turn out bad!!" Meaning, when they make bad choices.

I found it's easy to give my kids the credit for making good choices. But as a parent, I seemed to want to take all the blame when they made bad choices.

Another piece of wisdom my Dad passed along to me was, "If God himself can't change them, then what makes you think you can?" Of course, we know God can, but He gave them free will. He doesn't make them choose Him. He leaves them that choice. I heard a pastor say, "The only thing stronger than the will of God is the choice that He gave you." I call it "want to". I prayed that God would change their "want to", that they would "want to" follow

Christ, that they would "want to" read His word, that they would "want to" make good decisions. I prayed that they would choose Him. Then I knew I had to release them to the Lord and trust Him.

LETTING GO

I sensed the Lord saying to me, "Lori, let go, you're holding onto your children so tight that there's no room for me to work." I mean, I had a white-knuckle grip.

This reminded me of a field trip that Eden and I took with her eighth-grade class to Washington, D.C. Part of the field trip involved a rock-climbing wall. I am not afraid of heights; I am mortified of heights! Now I don't know how I allowed the group I was in to get that harness on me and talk me into climbing up that wall, but it happened. Before I knew it, I had climbed to the very top of the rock wall. Then the horrifying realization came to me: *what goes up must come down.*

I had a white-knuckle death grip on that rock, and as I was clinging to the wall at the top, I heard a voice from below yell: "Now let go of the rock, grab onto the rope, and rappel down!" I was thinking, *they have lost their minds. I'm going to fall to my death.*

But there was no way I could continue holding onto that wall. My strength was giving way, I was losing my grip and I could not last. I had to let go so that I could grab onto the rope and rappel down to safety. With trembling arms, I finally let go of the rock and grabbed hold of the rope, landing safely at the bottom. Back on solid ground.

The Holy Spirit reminded me of this story several years later when I found myself again in a white-knuckle grip situation, but this time it wasn't about saving myself. It was about saving my daughter—not from falling off of a rock—but from falling into a bottomless pit of drug addiction and possibly her death. At this time in our lives, I thought if I didn't hold onto my children, they were going to die. How could I dare to open my hands and let go? I know that when we let go and grab onto God, He gives us the strength and power we need to bring us to that place of peace. I knew the Lord was saying, "I'm going to need you to let go of them and give them to me." As long as I had a tight grip on them, God couldn't work.

Now, how am I going to do that? These questions and thoughts flooded my mind. What in the world is going to happen to them? I am the one who has taken care of them their whole lives. They won't make it without me, without Super Mom.

I sensed the Lord telling me to pray over their lives, "Have Your will and Your way in their lives, no matter what it takes." Have you ever had to wrestle with God? I felt like I was entering the ring for the wrestling match of my life . . . like WWE Smackdown. Knowing I was going to lose yet ultimately win. There is victory in surrendering to God's will and way. It reminds me of the story of Jacob when he wrestled with Jesus, and he got his hip dislocated. We read there in Genesis 32 that Jacob grabs hold of Jesus and tells him that he will not let Him go until He blesses him. Before the blessing, Jacob sustained a lifelong limp that day that would remind him to lean and let God lead. Often God has to break us before He can bless us to teach us that we will aways need to lean on Him. We can't do it on our own. He doesn't break us to destroy us but rather to lead us into our destiny, the plan He has for us. We need to do life leaning on the everlasting arms.

As crazy as this may sound, at this point in my wrestling, I felt the need to talk back. I needed some serious clarity. Now Lord, you want me to do what? Let me make sure I'm hearing You right. You want me to ask You to have Your will and Your way in my children's lives no matter what it takes? His reply was simply, "yes." "I don't know if I can do that Jesus. I'm going to need a whole lot of help with this one. Jesus, I don't even know where to begin or how to do this. Oh, God please help me," I cried out to Him. God is Sovereign and Holy and must be respected, but He can handle our questions and the need to wrestle with Him to work some things out.

It was at this very moment that I realized I didn't trust Jesus! This was a scary revelation to dare to admit after knowing Jesus most of my life. If you had asked me about my Christian walk and if I had faith and trusted in the Lord, I would have had no doubt or hesitation to answer "yes!!!"

I not only talked about and claimed to have faith—you could find me every Sunday morning in church raising my hands, singing and proclaiming through worship from the bottom of my soul "My hope is built on nothing less than Jesus's blood and righteousness!" I was kind of skipping over the second part that says, ". . . all other ground is sinking sand."

As Christians, we sing about faith, talk about faith, and even brag about faith. However, it is not faith until it's tried and tested. The Bible talks about the fire that refines us. After assessing the condition of my soul, I don't think there would have been enough gold to come out of that refining fire that I was in to cover even one gold tooth on the rapper Lil Wayne! I had a Jesus + me kind of relationship with Him. Jesus definitely didn't need my help, but I absolutely needed His. He wanted my obedience. I've heard it said, "When we act on what we see, that's obedience. When we act on what we can't see, that's faith!!"

IN THE ARMS OF JESUS

Now that I realized I had idols in my life and I didn't trust Jesus, I began to wonder if I even knew Jesus at all. Was I even saved? Was I really a Christian, a follower of Christ? My world was crumbling into a million pieces.

During this time, it was also revealed to me that, I was not, in fact, Super Mom. I was full of pride. Self-righteousness was at work. My plan was to raise my little baby dolls—my I-Dolls—to be the next Mother Teresa. We need to trust God's grace to write our children's own testimony. Sometimes, Satan blinds us from the truth so we can remain in our sin. In my mind, there was absolutely nothing wrong with what I was doing. The goal was to raise "godly girls". Nothing was wrong with that. After all, wasn't that what God wanted for them? Yes, but in His will and His way. My job as their mom was to seek first the kingdom of God and His righteousness (Matthew 6:33, KJV).

The crazy thing is I always saw myself as a humble person. "Prideful person" would have never crossed my mind. The Bible has a lot to say about pride, "When pride comes, then comes disgrace, but with humility comes wisdom" (Proverbs 11:2), and "Pride goes before destruction, a haughty spirit before a fall" (Proverbs 16:18). I was in need of a spiritual heart transplant. The only way this was going to happen was through Jesus. I prayed these Scriptures over my life and my children. I prayed "Create in me a pure heart, O God, and renew a steadfast spirit within me. Do not cast me from your presence or take your Holy Spirit from me. Restore to me the joy of your salvation and grant me a willing spirit, to sustain me" (Psalm 51:10-12). I needed to trade my will for God's will. I began to spend more time with Jesus, in prayer and reading His word. Prayer is communicating with Jesus, not only you are talking but taking the time to listen. I always say, "If you need strength, get you some joy; if you need joy, get in God's presence." I based that thought on these two Scriptures "…Do not grieve for the joy of the Lord is your strength" (Nehemiah 8:10) and "In Your presence is fullness of joy" (Psalm 16:11, NKJV). I believe that the Bible is the inerrant Holy Word of God, and that He is the only way and the only truth. His Word became life for me. I definitely needed some joy and to be in His presence abiding in Him.

Jesus began to show me through the Bible, spending time in prayer and sensing what He was speaking to my spirit, that I needed to let go and release my children to Him. I wish I could tell you that I got right down on my knees in repentance but, sadly, I didn't. I was totally fear-driven at this point in my life. I didn't want to let my children go. I knew if I said those words, if I released my children to God, there were no limits. That meant they could be marred, maimed, arrested, or even killed. The good of what could happen by releasing them to the Lord didn't cross my mind. My fear interrupted any faith with bad thoughts. I wrestled with this for a while.

Finally, I came to the end of myself—a desperate woman, a desperate mother, with a desperate cry for help. That desperation was the sound of me falling to my knees in the middle of my living room floor and sobbing. I had gone to my upstairs living room. I felt the presence and power of the Lord: a warmth, a peace, a comfort, a reassurance, and a strength all in that moment. Jesus was literally meeting me there, right where I was so broken. I knelt down and closed my eyes, and I could see Jesus as He came with outstretched arms and knelt right in front of me as I took my children's lifeless bodies—and that's what they were as long as I held onto them with that "death grip". One by one I took them from my arms and placed them into the arms of Jesus. I could see His arms taking them from mine and I prayed, "Lord have your will and your way in their lives no matter what it takes." To be honest, at first, I could not say those words. I felt like I could not even breathe. I felt like I wanted to throw up or pass out at the same time. This was a huge step I was taking and only God could give me the faith and courage to take it.

By God's grace, I was able to pray this prayer over each one of my children. The minute I prayed this and handed them over, I felt a peace flood my soul. My circumstances weren't necessarily changed in that instant, but I was, I knew I could trust Him because no matter what, He was in control of my life, and with that came peace.

We do not have the power to change others; all
we have is the choice to let God change us.

He has taught me to trust Him with everything. Do I have to be reminded? Yes, sometimes daily. Paul says ". . . That is why, for Christ's sake, I delight in weaknesses, in insults, in hardships, in persecutions, in difficulties. For when I am weak, then I am strong" (2 Corinthians 12:10). It's easy to boast about our strengths so others can see how good we are doing. But to actually boast in our weaknesses is a real challenge—to admit we don't have it all together and we don't have it all under control—but it's during these weaknesses that Jesus can shine the brightest in our lives. When I finally acknowledge that I am weak, that's when I can make it through the power and strength that comes from Jesus. All the glory belongs to Him.

I feel this can be summed up in a quote by Joni Eareckson Tada, who became a quadriplegic in her teens as a result of breaking her neck in a diving accident. She writes "My weakness, that is, my quadriplegia, is my greatest asset because it forces me into the arms of Christ every single morning when I get up. Sometimes God allows what He hates to accomplish what he loves."[4]

We do not have the power to change others; all we have is the choice to let God change us. Sometimes we get so caught up and sidetracked in what God needs to do in our spouse or our children or another when all He needs us to do is give them or that situation to Him and focus on what He is trying to teach you. He loves us too much to leave us like we are—hopeless without Him.

---

4   https://www.brainyquote.com/quotes/joni_eareckson_tada_526378

CHAPTER 8

Pregnant and living in a Shed

> *For You created my inmost being; you knit*
> *me together in my mother's womb.*
> —PSALM 139:13

THE NIGHT I MET "THE BOYFRIEND"

*L*ate one cold February night in 2011, I heard a knock at the door. It was Eden. Standing beside her was a man I had never seen or met since I knew very little about Eden's life during this time. I opened the door and Eden stepped in and asked to borrow an electric heater and a blanket. I stood there thinking, *this is an odd request.*

The man stepped inside with her and stood right by the door. Eden said, "Mom this is Donnie; Donnie, this is my mom, Lori." I looked into his eyes and was taken aback. I'm not sure how to describe it; I had seen darkness before, but this somehow seemed darker. I had never experienced anything quite like it. I was trying to be nice but at the same time, I was sort of frozen in my tracks and could not stop staring at him. It was like everything stopped. We didn't move. It was so awkward, even scary. This verse came to me again, "The eye is the lamp of the body. If your eyes are healthy, your whole body will be full of light. But if your eyes are unhealthy, your whole body will be full of darkness" (Matthew 6:22-23).

Eden broke the silence and the staring when she looked at me with disgust and said, "Mom!"

I didn't know what to say or do. I felt uncomfortable like the presence of evil and didn't really want that in our house. I have never responded to anyone that way. It had taken me by surprise, and I wasn't sure what I needed to do.

He seemed to sense that I was uncomfortable. So, he told Eden he would just wait outside and stepped back out on the porch.

I gave her the blanket and heater that she had asked to borrow and just like that she was gone again.

Another request to add to the prayer list. I began to fervently pray for God to remove this man from Eden's life. Sadly, at that time, I had not even considered that he needed Jesus, too.

I'm by no means making my daughter out to be innocent, but this was not the daughter I knew and raised. She had somehow allowed this darkness into her own life. All I knew was that I needed God to rescue my daughter.

PREGNANT AND ON METH

The day after Eden had stopped by our house, my daughter Lindy came over to tell me that Eden was pregnant. A million thoughts rushed through my head. I told Lindy about giving Eden the blanket and heater the night before and that's when she proceeded to tell me that the reason Eden needed these items was because she was living with that guy, Donnie, in a shed. It was then that I learned that the man I met the night before was her boyfriend and that he was in a gang—one I had never heard of, but would soon find out—a violent one.

Now, I was not only in a spiritual battle for the life of my daughter but also for the life of my first grandbaby. Terrible thoughts plagued me. It was devastating to think what would happen to my grandbaby knowing the life my daughter was living.

I didn't think it was possible, but I prayed even harder, reminding Jesus that I gave her to Him. He already knew. I think I was actually trying to remind myself at that moment. I would speak out loud, "God, they are yours." My Dad would always tell me, "Children are a gift on loan from God."

DESPERATION HAS A SOUND

I did not want my daughter to be pregnant, especially under these circumstances, but I had to put things in perspective. The fact that she was still alive made me feel like we could handle pregnancy if she would just come home.

Have you ever been desperate for God to change your situation? I was absolutely desperate. Desperation has a sound. As I read about these women in God's word, I could hear their desperation. For Jochebed, the mother of Moses, it was the sound of ripples in the water as she placed her three-month-old baby in a basket and watched it float down the river, not knowing what would happen.

For Hannah, it was the silent cry from the agony of her soul as she knelt at the altar, begging God for a baby. The Bible says her lips were moving but her voice was not heard. But God heard.

For Sarah, it was the sound of her nervous laughter in unbelief as she was told that she would finally have a baby at ninety years old.

For the woman with the issue of blood, it was the sound of her dragging her weakened body through the dirt just to be able to touch the hem of Jesus's garment.

For the woman at the well, it was, "Give me living water that I may thirst no more."

And for me, it was screaming and sobbing into my pillow some nights, begging God to please save my daughter and grandbaby. On other nights, there was no sound at all; I was unable to speak . . . just breathless silence from this mother's heartbroken, silent cry, screaming from my soul with no words coming out.

I was what I call "soul sick". That's the only way I can describe my state. At night when I got in bed, tears flooded my pillow as I whispered "Jesus, Jesus, Jesus." I literally had to ask God for what I had always taken for granted . . . sleep. Sometimes when I felt like I had no words, I would ask Jesus to please put it on somebody else's heart to pray.

Two scriptures supported me during this time when I didn't have words to pray: Jesus ever lives to make intercession for us (See Hebrews 7:25, author paraphrase) and "In the same way, the Spirit helps us in our weakness. We do not know what we ought to pray for, but the Spirit himself intercedes for us through wordless groans" (Romans 8:26). These words gave me great comfort in knowing I have Jesus and the Holy Spirit interceding in heaven's throne room on behalf of me and my daughters, especially when I felt I had no words left.

Before I heard the news that I was going to be a grandmom, I would always say, "I hope it will be a while before I have grandchildren." After raising four children, I felt like I needed a break. And even though my youngest was nineteen and heading to college, I felt like I wasn't finished raising my own. Children should not be having children. They needed a little age and maturity first, and of course, a godly, responsible husband. I learned real quick You can't always get what you want. The older my children got, the more I realized life happens. Many things are out of our control, and we are just left to deal with it when they get to make their own choices. Remember, she now holds all the pennies.

"MOM, I DON'T NEED YOUR HELP"

So I not only felt desperation as a mom but now as a grandmom . . . which in just a few short months would be "GG"!

Just a few days after I found out that Eden was pregnant, she stopped by our house. I can't remember why she came, but I do remember her walking upstairs where I was doing some Bible reading. She had been there for a short while and had not mentioned being pregnant, so I told her that I knew. She really had no response, other than that look with her squinted eyebrows that she often gave me. I continued by saying,

"Eden, you need to see a doctor. Let me take you to the doctor. Do you want me to help you?"

"No, I don't need your help."

"Eden," I pleaded. "You can't be pregnant on drugs. It will hurt the baby."

"No, it won't," she said. She went on to tell me how a "friend" of hers who had kids had told her she could wean herself off meth while she was pregnant and that it would not hurt the baby. She was hard and angry and did not want to hear anything I had to say.

Finally, I said, "Eden, don't listen to me, and don't listen to your friend. Please go to an OBGYN doctor and whatever they tell you about meth and pregnancy will be okay with me because they're the experts."

She walked out that day, and I had no idea what would happen to her or my grandbaby.

PRAYERS

I had no idea how God was going to answer all those prayers, but we were sending them up. Little did I know things were going to get a whole lot worse before they got better.

———————————

I don't know what is going to happen this

very second, much less tonight or tomorrow,

but I do know who holds my present

and tomorrow and who holds me.

———————————

Jesus tells us "... In this world you will have trouble. But take heart! I have overcome the world" (John 16:33). He didn't say you "may" or "if" you have trouble, He said you "will." We not only have to trust that God will answer our prayers; we have to trust the way He goes about it. God is sovereign (supreme power or authority), omnipotent (having unlimited power, able to do anything), omnipresent (present everywhere at the same time), and all-powerful! He sees the whole picture.

I don't know what is going to happen this very second, much less tonight or tomorrow, but I do know who holds my present and tomorrow and who holds me. Life can change in an instant. Isaiah 55:8-9 says "For my thoughts are not your thoughts, neither are your ways my ways, declares the LORD. As the heavens are higher than the earth, so are my ways higher than your ways and my thoughts than your thoughts." So I choose to put my trust in God, my Father, the only true God.

EDEN'S PERSPECTIVE

My boyfriend, Donnie, and I lived in a shed behind his granny's house in Mobile, Alabama. I'm talking about a literal shed in the middle of winter with no heater. Even though it was tiny, we had a single mattress on a wooden platform on the concrete floor, a recliner, a few

The shed

shelves, and even a TV. There was electricity but no bathroom or running water.

Since we didn't live with our "dope" cook anymore, we decided we would start cooking it ourselves so that we would have enough to stay high and make enough money to get the supplies to make more.

Although I said "I never will" at this point in my addiction, I started shooting up. I was looking for that "bigger high". I couldn't do it myself because I hated needles and blood, but in the drug world, there was always someone there willing to do it for you.

About a month into living in the shed, we were getting high when one day I realized that the high didn't last very long. I remembered this girl had told me one time that that was how she found out she was pregnant—because she wasn't able to get high anymore. I told Donnie. The next day he went to buy a pregnancy test. When he came back, I went inside his granny's house to use her bathroom to take the test, hoping it wasn't positive. I walked out to the shed with the pregnancy test and handed it to Donnie. It was positive. He was happy, but I was not happy at all. A baby wasn't part of the plan. This meant that I was going to have to stop doing drugs, and I didn't think that was possible. If you've never dealt with drug addiction, this is probably impossible for you to understand. It's like your body craves drugs more than life itself and you literally do not care about anything else.

Eden & Mary Kathryn with Dad

Me, Eden, and baby Noah

Noah and GG

Noah and Papaw

Lindy, Mamaw, Shane, me, Noah, and Eden

Noah and mom

Lindy, baby Emberlee, Kristin, me, Mary Kathryn, Eden

Lindy, Eden, Mary Kathryn, Kristin "squeezing"

CHAPTER 9

What Can Happen in Six Days?

*For I am the Lord your God, who takes hold of your right hand
and says to you, Do not fear; I will help you.*
Isaiah 41:13

DETECTIVES IN MY LIVING ROOM

A lot can happen in six days. This is how it started for me. In March 2011, I got up and went to work at 6 a.m., as usual. I was working as a nurse at a local hospital. That day when I went on my break, I took my cell phone out of my locker and noticed that I had a missed call from my Mom with a voicemail saying, "Call me." My Mom rarely called me at work, so I immediately called her back. She told me that Eden's boyfriend Donnie had been arrested. We had been praying for God to take him out of her life because they were in drug addiction together. We were desperate for Eden to get off of drugs, come home, and save herself and her baby, so we thought getting away from him was part of the answer. Although we did not wish Donnie ill, it seemed like an answer to prayer for us to get him away from her—but this wasn't the end of the story. It was only the beginning.

My Mom said Detective H. wanted to talk with Eden about a homicide investigation. I said wait. . . . did you say homicide? Did Donnie kill somebody? Is that why he got arrested? Mom said, "I don't know, but the Detective left his card." I said, "Okay, I will see about all of this when I get home," and we ended the call.

I had no idea what was going on. All these questions raced through my mind as I finished my shift at work. "Who was killed?" "Why did Donnie get arrested?" "Where is Eden?" "Where is Lindy?"

At this point, Eden was about five weeks pregnant. My racing mind and my praying heart seemed to be in competition with one another. We all have this promise from God in Isaiah 26:3, "You will keep in perfect peace those whose minds are steadfast, because they trust in You." I needed peace, but would I choose to keep my mind on the problem or steadfast on the problem solver, Jesus? You have to remember in all of this that God was doing a work in me. I had a battle going on inside of myself to solidify my faith to leave my children in God's hands and trust His ways.

I came home from work that night; my parents did not have any new information, so I went to bed and could barely sleep. I had no idea what was going on, but I knew it must be bad. I spoke to the detective the next day and he said he would be back out at our house to meet with me. Before this happened, I called our attorney, Michael Newton, to try to help me figure this out. At that time, we really didn't have enough information to know what was going on. We got together with my youngest daughter, Mary Kathryn, and asked her to call Lindy and Eden to see if she could meet up and talk with them. We thought that possibly she could get more information so we could know what to do. Even though she didn't have much to do with them at this time in their lives, they would usually still respond to her calls. Mary Kathryn called and went to meet with them. She came back and said they were really messed up on drugs. She told us that she was scared and just wanted to get away from them. I was sorry we had asked her to meet with them. I was so upset and not thinking things through, just reacting in fear instead of responding in faith. The truth is I had no idea what to do.

Detective H. returned to our house with a police officer this time to meet with me about the homicide investigation and the whereabouts of Eden. He stated that he needed to talk to her again. The Detective told me that he had picked my daughters Eden and Kristin up from the motel. This particular motel has a reputation for prostitution and drugs. He went on to say that they picked up several other people with my daughters at this motel to question them in regard to a murder investigation, but he had let them go. I said, "You questioned who?" He repeated, "Eden and Kristin." Looking at him puzzled and confused, I asked, "In Minnesota"? He said, "No, I questioned her here in Mobile." I said to him, "My daughter Kristin lives in Minnesota." At this point, I told the Detective that he had the wrong daughter. I explained to him that it was in fact Lindy that he had questioned and released. I knew Lindy must have used her sister Kristin's name to keep from getting arrested. She had done this in a prior arrest. I found out later that is exactly what she did because she already had an outstanding warrant for VOP (Violation of Probation). Lindy had struggled with drug addiction for years and had been in and out of jail and probation many times. She had also been to several rehabs but always went back to drugs.

I know the Detective was not happy when he realized Lindy had used false information to avoid arrest, although he did not acknowledge being upset with Lindy at this time, he certainly took care of it with a warrant when he left.

While in our home, Detective H. went on to say, "Eden is just a young girl who got messed up with the wrong people." I said, "Yes, she has lost her way and to add to all of this, she is pregnant with my first grandchild." He said, "She is not in trouble or wanted; I just need to know what she knows in connection with the homicide." He then said to me, "I don't want your daughter; I just need to ask her some questions." I asked, "Who was murdered?" He told me the guy's name and explained that it was gang-related. We ended our meeting with me telling him that if I see or hear from Eden, I will let him know.

A WARRANT FOR LINDY

Detective H. left my house that morning and issued a new warrant for Lindy for giving a false name to an officer. The US Marshals then showed up to the motel to arrest Lindy for using a fake name. While they were there, they obtained a search warrant and searched the motel room that Lindy and her boyfriend,

Greg P., had been staying in. Inside this room, they found a meth lab and charged both Lindy and Greg P. with manufacturing methamphetamines.

Lindy called me first thing after she got to jail and through the booking process. The phone calls were limited, so she started by saying, "Mom, I need you to just listen." She was talking ninety miles a minute. She began to explain to me what was going on and that I needed to find Eden because Stan had taken her somewhere and she did not know where, but she believed Eden's life was in danger. Lindy also said that this guy that has Eden is also in the same gang as her boyfriend, Donnie, and that they had all been staying together at the motel.

Seems like things were going from bad to worse, and my fear was, too. I called my work at the hospital, spoke to my nurse manager, and explained to him that I needed a few days off. Thank the Lord I had a great manager who understood and told me that he would be praying and to do what I needed to do for my family.

DETECTIVES BACK IN MY LIVING ROOM AGAIN

Detective H., along with another officer, made their third visit to our house. At this time, he had not been able to find Eden, so he seemed a little more agitated on this visit. He reiterated that he was looking for Eden for questioning in this serious homicide investigation. He stated again that he was "not looking to charge Eden, he just needs information from her." I let him know that I understood that, but I did not know where she was and had not seen or heard from her. I assured him we had all been trying to get in touch with her but had been unsuccessful.

He never came right out and accused me, but it seemed as if he thought I was hiding my daughter or at least knew where she was and just wasn't telling him.

By the time this visit with the Detective took place, I knew Lindy had been arrested and I had already spoken to her and knew a little more about what was going on. I let him know at this point that I had not spoken to Eden and that I did not know where she was, but the last I heard was that she was with Stan. I told him that they needed to find her because I felt like her life was in danger. I let him know that I was making phone calls and looking for her myself.

The Detective and I discussed the fact that this was a gang-related murder. He said that I didn't need to be afraid because this gang is not dangerous; they don't go around just killing people. I then said, "I'm sorry, sir, but isn't this why you're sitting in my living room—because a man has been murdered by this gang? And frankly, I don't want my daughter to be next."

Before this meeting with the Detective, I had done a little research on this gang and found out that they are indeed dangerous, full of anger and hate. I read they are a neo-Nazi prison gang and an organized crime syndicate and the most notorious racist prison gang in the United States. They are known for activities of murder, assault, drug trafficking, robbery, gambling, extortion, and racketeering. Shock is not the word. When I read all of this my mind was racing with all kinds of thoughts, like *how can this be the father of my grandbaby, where is Eden, are they going to kill her, are they going to kill us?. . . .* the questions went on and on. My mind was spinning like a sprayed roach! (Ya probably have to live in the south to understand that statement.) Trying to take all these thoughts captive was difficult, I then tried to express to the

Detective the importance of finding Eden before she was the next victim; in fact, I wanted them to find her more than they did. I felt in my gut that her life was in danger. I was terrified that this guy from the gang that had her was going to kill her. I went on to say to the Detective, "To be truthful with you, if my daughter is found alive, I certainly do not want her to testify against this gang." There was the potential for harm to her and our entire family. He then mentioned the Witness Protection Program. My response was, "We have a big family and there is no way you can protect all of us."

At this point, I really couldn't be concerned with all of that. I just wanted to find Eden. I began to pray for protection over Eden and our entire family. This was way bigger than me; we needed Jesus's protection—not witness protection!!!

MOM ON A MISSION WITH A .380 SEMI-AUTOMATIC

So now we are all aware that Eden is pregnant and missing. I started trying to find her. We all called and called her cell phone, but no answer. I called, Mary Kathryn called, her sister Kristin called, but she did not answer. My heart sank. I did not know if Stan had killed her.

What is a mom to do? I would like to tell you that I immediately fell on my face before God full of faith knowing that He had everything under control. I am so glad that I serve a God who is compassionate, gracious, slow to anger, and abounding in love (See Exodus 34:6).

I knew I had to do something. I grabbed a picture of Eden, along with my .380 handgun, and headed out determined to find my daughter.

Desperation has a sound, the sound of snatching a picture frame from the wall, pulling the back off, and grabbing a picture of Eden out of that frame, not stopping to pray, but more or less "panic praying" as I went out of my front door.

I did not have a clue where to begin looking and Lindy was in jail so she couldn't help me. I had heard of "drug motels" in Theodore and Mobile, but I did not know where they were or which ones I should search, for that matter. But I had to start somewhere.

Just as I was leaving my house, my cell phone rang and it was one of my best friends, Debby—that "ride or die" friend. She wanted an update, and I told her what I was going to do. She said, "That is not safe." I said, very sternly, "I am going to find my daughter." "Well then I'm going with you, so come get me," she said.

I left the house, swung by, picked her up, and began driving around looking for what we thought were "skank" motels. We went from motel to motel. She stayed in the car, and I would get out with the gun tucked in my pants, under my shirt, and the picture of Eden. I was gonna go "Madea" on somebody! I would go into these motels, show the photo of Eden, and ask, "Have you seen this girl? She's my daughter." I heard over and over the same disheartening reply . . . no, no, no. The devastation, fear, and despair I felt that day are beyond words.

At that moment we didn't know

if Eden was dead or alive.

After searching for a while, I called my youngest daughter, Mary Kathryn, to go help me look for Eden. Mary Kathryn was at a friend's house, so I went and picked her up. Like me, most of the time Mary Kathryn didn't know where her two sisters were, nor did she have much communication with them, but I knew they would talk to her sometimes when they wouldn't talk to me. But at this time, Eden wasn't answering any of our phone calls.

I was out of options. Our last stop seemed like the bottom of the barrel, the motel. As I said, this motel is not a safe place. It is known for prostitution and drugs. Definitely not a place you would ever want to find your kids. We had just pulled in when these men began walking toward my car. They were wearing black with what looked like black army boots. In my mind, I figured they must be in the gang and that must be how they dress. With my heart pounding, I reached down to grab my gun from under the front seat. Instantly, Debby reached down and grabbed my hand saying, "Lori, it's the police, put the gun down!" I thought they were from the gang that possibly had Eden. They were in fact, federal marshals! Somehow, I had failed to see the big shiny badge hanging around their necks. I guess the black clothing was their bulletproof vest. The place was covered with the Feds and the police. Officer G. approached my vehicle; I rolled the window down. I told him I was looking for my daughter Eden. He told me they were looking for her, too. I got out of my vehicle. The officer reached into his vest and pulled out a picture of my children. He asked me if they were my daughters. I said, "Yes." It was a picture of them that had been taken just seven months prior at Kristin's wedding.

At that moment we didn't know if Eden was dead or alive. We had called and called and sent many texts to her phone, over and over for two days with no reply.

We would find out later that Stan had not only taken Eden, but he had taken her cell phone and would not let her use it. We also heard that he was wanted for questioning in this same murder and that there were two different guns used and two different bullets were found in and around the man's body. Eden did not realize until later the potential danger her life was in at this point because to her, these were just her "drug buddies".

MORE THAN DRIVE-THRU JESUS

Finally, it dawned on me that trying to find Eden in a city the size of Mobile was like looking for a needle in a haystack. Finding her on my own was not going to happen. I needed more than "drive-thru Jesus". This was a war for the very life and soul of my daughter and grandbaby.

The Apostle Paul tells us, "For our struggle is not against flesh and blood, but against the rulers, against the authorities, against the powers of this dark world and against the spiritual forces of evil in the heavenly realms" (Ephesians 6:12). I had looked everywhere I could think of and could not find Eden, so I left the motel and went back home to do what I should have done in the beginning. I got down on my knees and gave it to Jesus. I guess "Annie Oakley" and her gun were not going to solve this one. And like Tyler Perry's "Madea", "I was not going to find peace with my "piece."

PRAYER CHAIN

God was all I had, but He was all I needed. Time and time again, He had proven to me to be more than enough in my life. Desperation has a sound, the sound of texting a group of my prayer warrior friends simply saying, "Please pray for Eden right now!" In this moment God reminded me that I had given her to Him, and that I needed to keep trusting Him.

I had no idea how God would use this to save her life as well as the life of my grandbaby. Eden's "return" wasn't anything like I had planned or imagined. There was no prodigal child knocking at the door, but within the hour of starting this prayer chain, the phone rang. As I answered the phone, it literally took my breath away when I heard my daughter's voice—it was Eden, she was alive! As we began to talk, she told me that she had been arrested about thirty minutes ago and was in jail. She went on to tell me about how she was hungry, so she stole some chicken wings from a grocery store deli! After comparing the time frame of the prayer chain and her arrest, we were blown away at the faithfulness of God. We were praying at the same time she was stealing chicken, not knowing that God was lining up a chain of events that would ultimately save her life. God can and will use anything to bring us back to Him, even a Chicken Wing and a Prayer. We read in God's word that we all, like sheep, have gone astray, but that Jesus, our good Shepherd, will leave the ninety-nine on the hills and go to look for the one that has wandered off. The Goodness of God is running after us.

GOD'S PERFECT TIMING

Once Detective H. realized that Eden was not going to risk her life, the life of her baby, or our family, to testify in the homicide case, he threw the book at her. At the beginning of this murder investigation, the police raided the shed where Eden and Donnie had been living, and they found drugs and a meth lab.

So much for all those conversations with the Detective in my living room about how they didn't want to arrest Eden. The Detective was no longer concerned about how "Eden was just a young girl who got mixed up with the wrong people." There is a part of me that understood that he had to do his job.

Eden was taken to Mobile Metro Jail. When she was given that first phone call, she called me. I had no idea what a mess she was in at this time. Now, two of my daughters were in jail. On one hand, my heart was broken, and on the other, relieved—thankful they were alive!

Jesus can always do things so much better than we think we can if we'll just give it all to Him and trust.

Going to jail was nowhere close to my plan of how Eden's life would be spared and brought back to Jesus. The prodigal daughter coming home knocking on the front door sounded a whole lot simpler to me, but God knew what was needed in Eden's life. Over the years God has taught me to expect Him because He is always there and always working. He also had to teach me to not set my expectations based on how He works, or the way or method in which He accomplishes His purpose. My part is to trust Him.

EDEN'S PERSPECTIVE

This is how the six days started for me. My boyfriend Donnie, me, my sister Lindy, her boyfriend Greg P., a fellow gang member, Stan, and his girlfriend Carla were all staying at the motel together. Our common bond was drugs. On March 18th, Detective H called

Donnie and asked him to come down to police headquarters for questioning in a homicide investigation. Stan drove Donnie, me, and Carla to the Mobile Police Precinct and parked across the street. When Donnie got out of the car, I began crying hysterically as my mind raced with many questions. I had just recently found out I was pregnant, and this was the father of my child. I said to him, "Promise me that you are not going to leave me." He promised, but we both knew this was a promise he would probably not be able to keep.

Eden's mugshot and after

Stan got out of the car and said he was going to watch to see if Donnie would be released after questioning. Me and Carla took the car and left because it was time to pick her two little girls up from school. After we got the girls, we started driving back to the shed where Donnie and I were living at the time. As we rounded the curve, we saw that the place was covered with police. They were there searching the shed. My heart started pounding. We pulled into a neighbor's driveway and turned around hoping the police would not notice us.

We immediately called Stan. He told us to come back and pick him up. When we arrived, he told us that Donnie had been detained in Mobile Metro Jail. I was so upset. We did not know what to do.

We took Carla's girls to an arcade in the mall to occupy them so we could figure out what to do. We decided it was best to take the girls to Carla's parents' house. After we dropped them off, we went back to the motel. My sister Lindy and her boyfriend Greg P. were there, and we told them what had happened. We all stayed there that night.

The next day, Stan, Carla, and I left the motel and walked across the street to the Dollar General to pick up some things. When we began walking back to the motel, a black SUV pulled up behind us really quickly. No one got out. I was relieved but scared. We went back to our motel room. We had not been back long when we decided to leave again, but as soon as we stepped outside, we were surrounded by task force officers with guns drawn.

"GET DOWN ON THE GROUND! GET DOWN ON THE GROUND!" they shouted. I have never been so scared in my entire life. I was so scared, I actually peed my pants. They began to search the hotel room, but they didn't have a search warrant so they couldn't continue their search. They had me, Lindy, Greg P., Stan, and Carla sitting on the curb in handcuffs. Approximately thirty minutes later, the detectives came and put me and my sister Lindy in the back of the same patrol car together. This was new to me; other than a DUI, I had never been in big trouble and had no idea how any of this worked. The lady detective said, "We just need to take y'all down to the station and ask a few questions." Puzzled, I asked, "You're going to bring us back here after that, right?"

I had never been questioned like this before and definitely never interrogated for a murder! During this interrogation, I was really high on drugs and very scared and confused. The detectives asked me about drugs in the shed and about the murder. I told them I had helped purchase some supplies to make the drugs. I did not have anything to do with the murder and did not want to be pulled into the middle of it. This was a crime involving an extremely violent gang. I was shaking with fear, and I wasn't going to put myself, my family, and my unborn child in that kind of danger. It was a known thing in the "drug world" not to snitch. I didn't want anyone in my family or me to be the next murder victim.

Stan, Greg P., and I were all arrested in order to be brought in for questioning regarding the murder. Lindy used a fake name, so she was let go. Greg P.'s sister bailed me and Greg P. out. We don't know how, but Stan and his girlfriend Carla were the only two that did not get arrested. They were actually released. We still don't know how that happened but those two were free to go.

After bail was posted, we left the jail. Stan immediately took my cell phone away from me and wouldn't allow me to call my sisters or my mom. He also would not let me out of his sight. He told me that I had to be with him or his girlfriend, Carla, at all times. I had no idea what was going on, but this should have set an alarm off in me. At this time, I wasn't afraid because, in my mind, I was with "friends".

We all went back to the motel and Stan got us another room that night. My sister and Greg P. were also staying there at the same motel again but in a separate room. Carla had fallen asleep, but I was upset and couldn't go to sleep.

I wanted to talk to my sister. Sometime later, I walked over to see Lindy and Greg P. in their motel room. I knocked, but no one answered the door. I went to the front desk to make sure I had the right room, and that's when I learned that Lindy and Greg P. had been arrested again. I hadn't heard anything and had no idea they had been taken into custody. I didn't know what to do. I was stuck here with Stan and Carla now that Donnie, Lindy, and Greg P. were all in jail. I went back to our room where Stan and Carla were, and I slept the rest of the night.

We got up the next day and headed out with no plan of where we were going. Carla and Stan were sleepy, so I drove us around for a few hours while they slept in the car. Later, after he woke up, Stan took over the driving. We aimlessly drove around all day. I was pregnant and really hungry, but Stan would not stop to get me anything to eat. I began to worry, just wondering *where are we going and what in the world are we going to do*? Stan stopped at one store where I went in and stole some beer for him. I figured if I got Stan some beer, he would eventually get me some food. We rode around a little longer and he finally pulled into a local grocery store so I could get something to eat. Hungry and broke, I went in and stole some chicken wings from the deli. I got back in the car and Stan started driving. He said he wanted some chicken, so I begrudgingly handed some to him, and he proceeded to eat it all. Just as he finished eating all the chicken, we stopped at a red light and he reached over to the backseat and handed me the trash with chicken crumbs. I was now starving and furious, so I rolled the window down and threw it all out on the side of the road.

Sitting next to us at that red light was a man in a big moving truck. He saw me litter and was obviously furious, as indicated in his voice, when he rolled his window down and yelled "If my son were here, he would fine you $500!" I was already annoyed, still hungry, and out of chicken. I just rolled my window back up and ignored him. He rolled his window back up as well.

But Stan wasn't letting it go. As we were waiting on the light to turn green, Stan opens his door yelling and cussing as he chucked an opened can of beer as hard as he could at that man's truck window. We immediately took off, and the man took off after us. As we were speeding down the road, we made a quick move and pulled into a strip mall. Our plan was to get out and act like we were just going in to do some shopping. No sooner than we had gotten out of the car, we were met face-to-face with a Mobile County Constable.

It just so happened that this Constable was there and the man in the truck flagged him down and he followed us into the shopping center. "I need to see your IDs," the Constable said. All three of us handed them over. When they ran my driver's license, the Constable said to me, "Ma'am, you are wanted on two outstanding warrants." "Me? For what?" I still did not know how all of this worked and had no idea that you could have warrants out and not know about them.

This arrest saved my life and the life of my unborn baby.

"Manufacturing and trafficking methamphetamines," the constable replied. When they searched the shed after Donnie was arrested, they found the meth lab and put out a warrant for my arrest. He read me my rights, placed me in handcuffs, put me in the back of his patrol car, and took me to jail. I was so afraid as thoughts of what was happening to my life raced through my mind. As I sat there, I thought, *why couldn't Stan have just kept his mouth shut and stayed in the car at that red light*?

While I was stealing chicken, my Mama and her friends were praying. Who knew that God would use a chicken wing and a prayer to lead to my arrest? But I'm thankful He did. This arrest saved my life and the life of my unborn baby.

CHAPTER 10

Life in Jail: The Redemption Story

*"When Jesus heard it, He said to them, "Those who are
well have no need of a physician, but those who are
sick. I came not to call the righteous, but sinners."*
MARK 2:17 (ESV)

MOBILE METRO JAIL

It broke my heart every time I drove by Mobile Metro Jail to know that my children were in there. You may think, "Lori they weren't children." No matter how old they get, they will always be my children. I didn't love them any less in their 20s than I did when they were infants.

When I would drive by the jail, I would always stretch my hand out toward the jail and pray for them. I remember one day after they had been in there for about two months, I got this bright idea to make big poster signs that said, "We love you, Eden and Lindy." My youngest daughter, Mary Kathryn, and I made the posters. We drove down to the jail. There was a side of the jail that had little, tiny windows that faced Interstate 10. We pulled off at that spot and got out of the car with the signs. We walked a little closer to the jail. As we stood there holding up these signs, we shouted, "We love you, Eden and Lindy!"

We had hoped that by chance they would look out that tiny window, see us, and feel a glimpse of hope and love. We found out later they never did. They had no way of knowing we were out there. I know this sounds crazy, but you feel desperate, even a little crazy, when your child is locked up in jail. I'm thankful the police didn't see us…they probably would have taken me to the psyche ward! I can just hear them now…"Ma'am put your little sign down because I'm gonna need you to come with us". God's got me…"The Lord watches over the foolish" (Psalms 116:6, NCV).

VISITATION AND PHONE CALLS

Visitation was strict. We had to make our appointment a week ahead of time for the visit. The day of the visit, we had to get there at least thirty minutes early and check in with our driver's license, and then we would sit and wait until they called us, which seemed like forever. Only two people could visit at once and it was usually me, my mom, and Mary Kathryn that would rotate. Your name had to be put on the visitation list by the inmate the week before your visit, and no changes could be made. The visit prohibited contact. There was a large glass window between the visitor and the inmate. The inmates would file in and sit down in chairs on each side of these small booths that were lined up in front of the glass. These booths were small sections partitioned off so that each inmate could visit with their family. We would spend each visit talking through a phone while looking through the glass at each other. Sometimes there was laughter and other times tears. I longed for the day I could hug and squeeze my daughters again. That's what we do in our family, we hug each other really, really tightly and we call it "squeeze"; we actually grit our teeth and say "squeeze it" as we are squeezing each other. Just a family thing.

There was something else I learned—the "books"—they are somewhat like a bank account for the inmate. The family deposits money so the inmate can buy stuff from what I call the "jail store"; they call it the commissary. And let me tell you, the jail store is expensive.

And another thing, in order for the inmate to make a phone call, the person they are calling has to have a "phone account" with the system in which you deposit money because phone calls from jail are not free—they're expensive too! My daughters would call me after lockdown at night. There were only two phones in the jail, so most often they had to wait in line. The call was timed for fifteen minutes, and it cut off right at fifteen minutes. It seemed like the shortest fifteen minutes of my life. We couldn't talk every day because it was way too expensive, but we talked at least once a week and sometimes twice.

OBGYN ASSIGNED, NOT PICKED

Eden didn't get to choose her doctor for her pregnancy; she was chosen for her. Dr. D. was the OBGYN doctor assigned to Eden while in jail— what a blessing from the Lord. Up to this point, Eden had not been to see her doctor. She had been sick, dealing with a UTI, dehydration, and fainting. She needed a doctor. I called the jail to speak with someone in authority who could make this happen. This was a big, secret thing when the guards would take an inmate to their doctor's appointment. Whether behind bars or taken out to the doctor, you were still an inmate, handcuffed and transported by the guards. The family could not know and were not allowed to go to any of her visits, but we did not know this rule, so we unknowingly broke it. Let me explain how this happened. Eden found out she was going to have a doctor's appointment, so she told us when and where it was going to be. We got up that morning so excited that we were going to see Eden and possibly hear the baby's heartbeat, but keep in mind we had no idea we weren't even supposed to know about this visit, let alone be there.

I had to trust that God had Eden where He needed

her, in a place where she could hear from Him.

We had not been at the doctor's office long when we found out what a big deal this was. We walked in and couldn't find Eden. We looked in the waiting room and couldn't find her. When we went to the check-in desk to ask about Eden the guard appeared and sternly told us that we were not supposed to know about this visit or be there. We were asked to leave, and the guard told us that our actions could have caused Eden to get an escape charge and be taken back to the jail without seeing her doctor. Eden had been sick, and I definitely did not want this to happen, and I certainly did not want her to get any more charges, she was in enough trouble on her own. We apologized and immediately left. Looking back, I somehow feel like we looked like the "Beverly Hillbillies" walking up in that waiting room that day like we were going to a baby reveal party. I'm sure the guard was thinking, Lord have mercy, this family is going to need some "Jail 101" lessons.

Eden called me later when she got back to jail to tell me all about the doctor's visit. She said she was brought to her appointment by a police officer in his car as well as a female corrections officer. She said, "It was so nice just to be in a car and see all the beautiful oak trees of midtown Mobile; I just remember feeling very grateful to get even a moment outside of that dark place." She said they brought her through the front door in shackles in front of everyone sitting in the lobby and the receptionist said to the guard, "Excuse me, you're supposed to take her through the back." Eden said that at that point, it was too late; there she was in front of everybody with chains and handcuffs.

The good news was that Eden was relieved to see the doctor that day and hear everything looked great. She got to hear her baby's heartbeat for the very first time. She said, "It was so surreal."

Looking back, I'm glad I missed the scene of my pregnant daughter in shackles at her OBGYN appointment. God was watching out for me.

It was hard to be forbidden from going with her to these doctor visits for several reasons. First, this was my daughter. I didn't want her to be alone at these doctor visits; after all, it was her first baby. Also, when you go from your daughter not wanting to be around you at all—like can't stand your guts—to now wanting your company, I didn't want to miss a minute of it.

Even though I really wanted to be with her to comfort her and share in the excitement, we both embraced the fact that a baby was on the way, regardless of the circumstances. I had to trust that God had Eden where He needed her, in a place where she could hear from Him.

PRAYER BRACELET: PRICEY VERSUS PRICELESS

I really like jewelry and definitely have more than I need. I was the last of five children in my family and my daddy always said, "The gypsies left you on our doorstep." I'm starting to believe him. All four of my daughters like jewelry too. My daughter Kristin especially likes it. She's a bit like what we call "froo froo", a little prissy. Maybe it's the gypsy blood coming out of her. My dad would call it "styling and profiling." Kristin is the sister in-between Eden and Lindy. She's a little ditzy but oh so cute. She should have been a blonde!!!

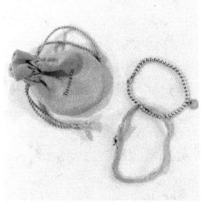

Prayer bracelet & Tiffany bracelet

My birthday was coming up that January. I think it was my forty-fifth. Kristin decided that I needed a Tiffany bracelet. These bracelets are a little pricey, so she spent several months prior to my birthday saving up to buy one for me—I didn't know her plan because she kept it a secret. When my birthday month arrived, I got this package in the mail. I opened it up to discover a little blue box. The color is actually called Tiffany blue. Those of you who are into jewelry already know that beautiful shade of blue is Tiffany's signature color. I was so excited. I had never gotten anything from Tiffany's. Inside this blue box was a tiny blue velvet Tiffany bag. Inside the velvet bag was a beautiful silver bracelet, with, of course, Tiffany's little signature heart on it! So excited, I put it on and called Kristin to thank her for my surprise. I wear it proudly with love from my daughter.

However, a few years later in April 2011, I got another bracelet—one I never dreamed I would wear. It did not come in a little blue box; it came in a plain white envelope. The envelope came in the mail from Eden while she was in jail. As I opened it up, I pulled out this little cloth bracelet along with a letter that read, "Mom, I made you this prayer bracelet out of some pieces of a torn, raggedy sheet here in jail. I want you to wear it to remind you to pray for me till I get home." With tears streaming down my face, crying "Oh God, please help my daughter," I put that bracelet on and did not stop praying or take it off until the day she was released from jail.

Here's the funny part, if there could be a funny part to this story. Eden had some red Kool-Aid she used to dye the bracelet red. I guess she wanted me to have a "fancy" prayer bracelet. The minute I took a shower, all the red washed off. I told her about it on our next call and we just laughed.

Although I appreciate my "pricey" Tiffany's bracelet, I can put no value on my prayer bracelet because it's "priceless" to me. Today, my prayer bracelet is in that little blue velvet bag from Tiffany & Co., locked up for safekeeping. "You are priceless to me. I love you and honor you" (Isaiah 43:4, NIRV).

Desperation has a sound. It's the sound of my daughter tearing a tattered sheet in jail to make a prayer bracelet saying, "Mom please pray for me."

No matter where your child is, no matter what your child has done, they need their mother's prayers. Never stop praying; never give up!

I have never been incarcerated—well, not behind literal bars—but I have been a prisoner to emotional pain, fear, shame, and unforgiveness, but Jesus has set me free. Below are some "jail tales", stories written by my daughters Eden and Lindy.

EDEN'S PERSPECTIVE

It is pointless for me to attempt to put into words an adequate description of the overwhelming devastation that consumes every part of you when you become incarcerated. No words can capture that exact feeling of desperate sorrow and fear. Honestly, I feared the gang more than I feared being in jail.

When I was arrested on March 23, 2011, they took me in for booking. I had my mugshot taken, I was fingerprinted, and then put in a cold holding cell for hours. I slept on and off while I was there.

Finally, they called my name, along with several other ladies to take us back to the general population. We had to be strip searched and then taken to the shower with a lice treatment shampoo as part of the requirements.

After I showered, I bagged my clothes up and turned them in to the officer where they would then be stored until my release. If you came in with a white bra, you were allowed to keep it on but if not, you would have to go without one under the jumpsuit they provided for you. I wasn't so lucky to have one on, but they did allow me to keep my underwear.

They handed me a mesh laundry bag and a thin foam mat that would be my bed for the duration of my time in jail. The corrections officer then walked us down through the halls, through locked jail doors, and into the wedge I would be staying in, Wedge B.

We sat at the steel tables until they assigned each of us to a cell. Upstairs in cell 104 is where they put me. At that time, I had three cellmates: Rena was on the top rack (bunk), Patty was on the bottom rack, and Dora was on the floor with her foam mat. The only place left for me was *also* on the floor. I put my disgustingly smelly mat with a thin tattered sheet down on the cold, hard cement floor with no pillow, laid down, and after a good cry, I fell asleep. Later on, I was given an old "itchy" blanket. I guess they didn't want us to get too comfy so that we wouldn't stay too long.

How can one illustrate the experience when reality slaps you in the face at 4:00 a.m. to get up for breakfast that next morning after spending your first night of many in jail? You are locked down in an 8"x10" cell with seven to eight other female inmates. Of course, there are only two steel bunks in each cell—you can do the math—somebody is going to be sleeping on the floor.

It was so crowded in this cell that at times my head would be directly beside the toilet where all these women would be up and down all night to pee or poop in.

As soon as my eyes opened the next morning, the horror of where I was set in as fear began to grip my heart with these thoughts screaming in my mind. "What if I never get out of this place?" "What if I have to stay here for the rest of my life?" "How will I survive in here?" "I can't do this! God, help me, please help me. I'm so afraid, Lord please help me, Oh God!"

I certainly felt like I couldn't do this and wouldn't survive those first few days or maybe even weeks after I was arrested. I can assure you, that even in the midst of my darkest hours, God still had His hand on me. He never left me. Even in those moments when I felt lonely and fear would try to take over my mind, telling me that "there was no way out and no hope for me now," the Lord was right there. He was there with me in the middle of the raging storm I faced every second of every single day. God is faithful, even when we are not. We can all count on that fact.

About a week after being in there, my cellmate Mena was released and gave me her Bible. My other cellmate, Dora, had been moved to another cell. Rena was now on the top rack, and I would be on the bottom. They did not want pregnant women on the top racks due to liability, nor were they supposed to even be in the cells upstairs, but for some reason, I was permitted to stay put.

We spent a great deal of time sleeping because there was nothing else to do besides read, try to watch the tiny TV, and listen to it above all the noise going on. Or, we could walk around the perimeter of the wedge.

There are no words to describe the stench. After a while, you have no choice but to get used to it. Except for the time this one inmate was brought in. I'm not sure why or what was wrong, but I've never smelled anything like it, and I literally threw up. She wasn't in our cell for long, but while she was there, we all shared a container of Bengay cream to put around and inside of our noses. I think I would have spent all the money my mom had put on my "books" to block that smell from my nose.

It took a few weeks of withdrawals for me to physically begin to function again, to have the strength to be able to get up off of that cold floor and start moving.

Crystal meth had been my life for the past eight months. I stayed high all day, every day. Now that I was incarcerated and no longer had methamphetamines, my body had to adjust for me to be able to live and function day to day without the drugs. Meth is a drug that keeps you up night and day. You don't sleep at all, so when you come off of it you sort of crash. You sleep for days.

Withdrawal from meth is not as painful as withdrawal from some other drugs, but you are not able to function normally or even be awake until it has worked its way out of your system. It usually takes a week or two.

In the beginning of the withdrawal, I pretty much felt like I was in a coma, only awake for very short periods of time. At the beginning of sobriety, you feel like you are starving every time your body wakes up. I ate whatever I could manage to get my hands on for about three or four minutes while awake, went to the bathroom, then stumbled back to wherever I could crash and fall back into that deep sleep of withdrawal again. This lasted a little more than a week.

One day, in the first week, as I was sound asleep and still detoxing, they called my name over the intercom, but I didn't hear them. My cellmates woke me up saying, "Hey is your name Metzger? They were calling you." They needed me to go down to the clinic. Routinely, when a new inmate comes in, they have to go down to the clinic for a urinalysis and a TB test.

I walked down the stairs and through the locked door into the holding space. Behind another locked door and up a step is the control room where the corrections officers would spend most of their shift so that they could see us from a heightened view and speak to us through the intercom. Also, inside this space was a holding cell which was used to house a higher-risk inmate at that time.

When I got down there, I began to feel really weak and sick. I sat down on the floor because I felt like I was going to faint.

Finally, the others caught up with us, so I managed to get up so we could get to the clinic. There was a line painted on the tile flooring which ran the length of the walls and was about two feet wide. The inmates were expected to walk within this line any time we were being taken somewhere.

When we got out into the hall and began to walk to the clinic, I started feeling lightheaded and dizzy again. Everything seemed to be going black, so I sat back down on the floor. This really irritated the C.O. (Corrections Officer). I slowly opened my eyes as the fainting feeling left me. It was as if I had blacked out and was coming to. "GET UP! GET UP! I KNOW YOU'RE FAKING IT! I SAW YOU OPEN YOUR EYES! GET UP!" So, I stood back up but instantly everything began to go black again. I told her, "I can't see! I am fainting and I'm pregnant!" She grabbed my arm and continued leading—more like pushing me in the direction of the clinic. At this point, I couldn't see anything. I have no idea how I even made it to the clinic.

Once we made it there, she began ordering me around. "STEP UP!" she barked. So, I lifted my foot up and started to try to step up on what I assumed was a step, but I couldn't see it. My foot did not land on a surface, so I continued trying to step up. I probably looked like a bull getting ready to charge with the way I was kicking my foot forward searching for some kind of step. "STEP UP!" STEP UP AND BACK!" Finally, my foot landed on the step of an exam chair where she lowered me to sit down.

A male nurse came in and I told him what was going on. He told me that I was severely dehydrated due to detoxing and almost to the point of needing IV fluids. At this point, I had been asleep for days without drinking a single drop of fluid. He did give me a tiny disposable cup of water and one refill. I drank that and he informed me that shifts were changing but someone else would be taking over and would make sure I was taken care of, but once he left, no one else actually cared. They took my urine sample and locked me in a holding cell for hours and never gave me any more water or anything. Once you're an inmate, it's like you're no longer a person to most of the people who have to deal with the inmates on a daily basis.

This wouldn't be the first time my medical needs were neglected during my stay in county jail. I was so worried that I was going to lose my baby from not getting proper medical care. When I got back to the wedge . . . let me explain. The cell block I was in was 900; it had two wedges—A and B. The wedge is an enclosed area that has six upper cells and six lower cells and a "day room" (or common area with tables for eating or sitting, playing cards, etc.) where we could hang out when we were permitted to be out of our cell. I called my mom to tell her what had taken place with me in the clinic that day. My mom was very upset and called the jail to put in a complaint, which led to me being taken to see the OBGYN.

Slowly but surely my strength began to come back, and I could stay awake for longer than five minutes at a time. I wanted to read, and all I had was a Bible that Mena had given me. It had been a long time since I had read the Bible. I began to read and talk to God again.

I lifted my hands, and I felt the Holy
Spirit rush over me like a wave.

The jail would allow ministries to come in and have "church" with the inmates every so often. Most of the time these ministries would meet in the chapel but occasionally, someone was brave enough to actually come into our wedge and we would gather around them at the steel tables, listening to worship music and a message of hope.

One day I was in my cell sleeping on my rack. I was awakened by a familiar song. Playing on that little stereo downstairs was the song "Praise You in the Storm". This song meant so much to me. The first time I heard it was in 2010. It helped me through some hard times when I was in the Home of Grace rehab center trying to get sober. It made me feel a closeness with the Lord.

When I heard this song playing throughout the jail, I immediately stood up and walked to the opening of my cell door. I lifted my hands, and I felt the Holy Spirit rush over me like a wave. I began to just sob and worship, declaring "Yes, Lord, I will praise you in THIS storm". After that song ended, I went back and sat down on my rack and began to reflect on my circumstances. It was at that moment that I gave my life back over to the Lord. I instantly felt lighter as I allowed him to take control again and lead me in the direction that He wanted me to go. I picked up that Bible that Mena had given me, and I read and read until bedtime. God had, in an instant, renewed in me a desire to serve Him and restore that intimate relationship we once had when I was a teenager. From that moment forward, I fully surrendered to God.

LINDY'S PERSPECTIVE

There were no words to describe the emotions that I felt the moment that I heard my pregnant little sister had been arrested. It was a combination of relief and sadness. I had been incarcerated many, many times over the years, but this was Eden's first real trip to the jail and possibly prison. I felt responsible for her being in that situation and my heart broke at the thought of her having to go through it all. The worst part of it was the fact that I had to look at her through a piece of plastic glass in the next wedge, which meant that I was not physically able to protect her and help her get through it. I was afraid that something was going to happen to her and the baby if she ended up in a bad situation with another one of the inmates.

So, in order to get to her wedge, I devised a plan. I was talking to one of the inmates in my wedge about my little sister being in the next wedge and how I really needed to get over there to where she was. She told me that the best way to move was to get into a fight, because then they would move me over to the other wedge. I had only been there for a few days and didn't have any problems with anybody. I did not think it was a good idea to just pick a fight. It wasn't a good idea to make any enemies when I was clearly going to be there for a long time.

So, this inmate decided that she would help me get moved by faking a fight with me and we did just that. We waited until everyone was out in the day room with us, and we started screaming at each other and pushing and choking each other. We made it look very realistic and the guards bought it. I have never been so happy to get in trouble with the guards in a correctional facility. Part of my "punishment" for getting into a fight was just what I wanted—to be with my sister. I was moved into the next wedge with Eden. We kept it a secret for a few months, but eventually, the entire jail knew we were sisters. We remained in the small wedge and cell together until just before Eden's release and I was moved due to overcrowding.

EDEN'S PERSPECTIVE

Psalms 4:8 (BSB) says, "I will lie down and sleep in peace, for You alone, O LORD, make me dwell in safety."

One day, we were on lockdown in our cell, waiting for head-count. This was a daily procedure when every inmate had to go to their cell and be locked down until the guards made their rounds to make sure every inmate was accounted for. After the headcount was over, it was just me and Lindy in our cell. I was lying on my bunk reading a book and Lindy was asleep on her mat on the concrete floor. Just after the iron bars opened, two other inmates rushed in and one of the girls began stomping Lindy's head, ribs, and stomach on the concrete floor. I jumped up off my bunk yelling for them to stop. The other girl shoved me back down on the bunk. I jumped up again, and she pushed me back down and looked toward my pregnant belly as she said, "If you know what's good for you, you will stay down, or I will kick you in your belly." I was terrified as I was forced to sit by helplessly, but I began to pray as they beat my sister. Then just like that, the beating stopped, and they ran out before the guards could see them. I was so afraid that they had caused head trauma or possibly even killed her because Lindy never budged or woke up. I immediately jumped up, ran over, and knelt down by her hysterically crying, "Lindy, wake up. Lindy, wake up. Are you ok?" Lindy slowly woke up, sat up, and said, "What's wrong?" She saw me crying and thought someone had hurt me. I told her what had happened. Crazy as it sounds, Lindy did not feel a thing and did not sustain any injuries. We looked her body up and down—not one scratch, bruise, or red mark was anywhere on her face or body. I was shocked and relieved. I was thinking, *there is no way that she couldn't be hurt as hard as that girl was stomping on her head*. It was as if the Lord put a protection around her. The Lord was definitely with us—our shield, our protector.

> *The Lord is my rock and my fortress and my deliverer, my God, my rock, in whom I take refuge, my shield, and the horn of my salvation, my stronghold. I call upon the Lord, who*

is worthy to be praised, and I am saved from my enemies.
— *Psalm 18:2 (ESV)*

God is so good even when we don't deserve it. That vicious attack that the enemy tried to use to bring us harm ended up being the very thing that God used to bring Himself glory.

We would pray, read, and put on the armor of God (See Ephesians 6) and pray it over our lives every night, just like my mom had taught us. These inmates all witnessed the power of God's protection over our lives.

I hope you never need to know this, but let me tell you how a Jailhouse Burrito is done. You buy hot Cheetos and ramen at the commissary. You take your bag of Cheetos and crush them up really finely. You crush the ramen up as well and put the pieces in with the Cheetos and the ramen seasoning all in the Cheeto bag. Then you add hot (aka warm) water in the bag about a half of the way full and mix everything up really well. Fold the bag up and let it soak all the water up to form a burrito. Then you tear the bag open down the middle to eat it. It's like a gelatinous texture and I was not a fan, but Lindy really liked them. We traded with each other for the extra food that we got on our trays. I wanted her vegetables, and she wanted my chips and cake.

The water didn't get very hot in the cell sink, but we used what we had to make it work.

The funniest part of this story is that when we were in the process of telling our mom how we made these burritos, she said, "Oh and you just put it in the microwave to cook it." We died laughing just at her thinking we had access to a microwave!!!

My birthday came just ten days after my arrest. This is how my cellmates made my birthday cake. They took cookies, scraped the icing out of the middle, and added water to make it a little runny, and then set it aside. Then they took the cookies and put them in the bag, crushed them up well, added a little water, and mixed it all together. They poured the mixture out in a bowl to firm it up and then added that delicious homemade icing on top, and there you have it—a homemade birthday cake!! Happy twenty-first birthday to me!

If you wanted to make it a little more special, you could crush up pieces of a candy bar or a snack cake, if you were lucky enough to have any, and add it to the mix.

LINDY'S PERSPECTIVE

The following story reminds me of when God parted the Red Sea and led the Israelites through safely on dry ground to help them escape destruction.

At Mobile Metro Jail, the men's and women's buildings were next to each other. Shortly after we had been there, I received letters from my boyfriend (at the time), Greg P.

Somehow, the main guard, we'll call her Ms. Guard, got word of this, searched me and confiscated the letters. Greg P. had used ugly racial slurs in his letter which made Ms. Guard very angry. It was apparent that she did not like us.

That day just before breakfast, she decided to read those hateful, racist words contained in that letter out loud over the intercom, telling everyone in there that the letter was for me and my sister. Making a guess, I would say the population in our jail at that time was probably five African-American inmates to every one Caucasian inmate, roughly thirty to forty inmates in total in our wedge. We knew we were in serious trouble.

We were so afraid and figured we were going to get badly beaten. When she read those horrifying words from that letter, it caused an upset from the majority of the inmates in our wedge. We could hear them talking about us, calling us Nazis and racists.

Eden and I both had what was called "special food trays", Eden's was because she was pregnant and mine was because I was experiencing blood sugar problems. The "special food" tray inmates were supposed to go first and get their lunch tray, but on this day, right after Ms. Guard read the letter, she opened every jail cell door but ours.

The inmates began to scream threats and violent obscenities at us as Ms. Guard allowed all these angry women to come out first so they could all jump us when we came out to get our trays. She then opened our cell door. We stood there, our hearts racing in fear as we tried to decide what we should do. Eden said, "Lindy, what do we do?" We both were thinking, *how can we protect Eden's baby?* I said, "We have to go out there and face it; we have no other choice; it's going to be worse for us if we don't."

We slowly stepped out of our cell. Normally the jail was very loud, but as we walked toward the door to where we were to pick up our "special trays," there was total silence. No one uttered a word. You could have heard a pin drop, as we both walked together directly through the middle of the room. Every single inmate moved back. It looked like the Red Sea was being parted for us as we walked right through the middle of all those women. No one laid as much as a finger on us; no one uttered a word. I know that the Lord made a way for us to escape destruction that day. We made it to the door, picked up our breakfast trays, sat down, and ate it in peace. The hand of God was surely on us.

Proverbs 16:7 (author paraphrase) says that when a person's ways please the LORD, He makes even their enemies to be at peace with them. We had set our ways to please the Lord.

EDEN'S PERSPECTIVE

The dark ugliness that we allowed in our lives during this time of rebellion and sin was regrettable. The truth is we are not racist; we were taught to love everybody, and that God loves everybody. Through the power of addiction, we chose to be around the men who were in these gangs. Many women were not only angry but hurt by those words that were read out loud that day, and for that, we are truly sorry. Through repentance and God's forgiveness and love, our hearts have been changed.

Ms. Guard, the one who read the letter that day, continued to show her disdain for us until the day my elderly grandmother came to visit. We were not allowed to have contact visits. Our visits took place in a space through a glass window with each of us holding a telephone used to communicate.

Lindy was sitting at the window visiting with our Mamaw who was in her eighties at the time. She tried to come every Saturday. On this day, Ms. Guard was on duty. As the visit was coming to an end, they announced "Five minutes left!" Mamaw had been sick and was going to the doctor that next week, so Lindy wanted to pray for her.

"Mamaw put your hand up on the glass," Lindy said, and Mamaw did. Then Lindy put her hand up on the glass as if to touch Mamaw's hand and she began to pray. I'm here to tell you my sister can pray. When the visit was over, Lindy walked by Ms. Guard who had just witnessed all this and she said, "Girl, you sure can pray." From that day forward, not only were we the apple of God's eye, but we were now Ms. Guard's favorites. This was the power of prayer.

When we chose to let God use us, even in the darkest hour of our lives, the freedom we found was indescribable. We started studying God's Word together and stood on His promises and truth. Because of our obedience, God was able to use us in a powerful way. We had become prayer warriors and we boldly proclaimed God's victory in every situation, at all costs. We were unashamed of our faith, and everyone knew it. We started a prayer list and we asked anyone who needed prayer to come to our cell, and we wrote their requests on a list that we kept posted up on our wall. We fervently prayed over these requests and came into agreement in the name of Jesus with those who were in need. We witnessed God's miraculous power over and over again in so many situations.

There was a woman named Tesa, whose mother was sick and had just been diagnosed with cancer. We prayed over her mother in faith that she would be healed. A few weeks went by and her mother had another doctor's appointment. After running several more tests, the doctors found that her cancer was gone, and no treatment was needed. That is the faithfulness of our God.

People from all over the facility would come to us and ask for prayer. We held Bible studies and sung songs of praise and worshipped in our cell. We didn't have music, so we made our own. My sister and I would sing a cappella. A sweet aroma of worship to our King.

I had been in jail for probably about a month. Lindy was in the cell with me now, cell 104. We had made it a point to pray every night, even our cell mates joined in, and we would take turns reading a passage in the Bible.

There is not a ton to do inside a county jail to keep your mind occupied, so reading and writing is something we did daily. My pregnant belly was visibly growing, and my baby was always on my mind. I started to make lists of baby names. A girl list and a boy list. I focused my efforts on boy names because in my heart I knew I had a baby boy coming. I prayed for God to give me the name that He would have for this little boy. Every name I had written down just didn't feel right.

One day, Lindy and I were discussing names and we got on the topic of biblical names. I definitely wanted his name to honor God, because I knew from the very beginning that he was a very anointed child. Finally, it hit me—God gave me the name Noah. I was in love. Now when we talked to him through my belly, we could call him by name. Lindy suggested Christopher as his middle name, and I thought, *wow, that's perfect*. Not only would that name reflect Christ, because the name Christ is literally in Christopher, but it would also be a gift to my mom to name him after her brother, whom she so dearly loved and had lost in 1989.

As I was reading my Bible one night, I came across Genesis 12:2-3. It reads, "I will make you into a great nation, and I will bless you. I will make your name great, and you will be a blessing. I will bless those who bless you, and whoever curses you I will curse. And all peoples on earth will be blessed through you." And I would end it by saying "Noah Christopher" to declare this over his life. I heard God whisper to my heart, "This is what I have planned for Noah." Now, not only did I have his God-given name picked, but now I had a declaration of prosperity to pray over him every single day. Lindy had also picked a very special verse just for Noah, "May He grant you according to your heart's desire, and fulfill all your purpose. We will rejoice in your salvation, and in the name of our God we will set up our banners. May the Lord fill all your petitions" (Psalms 20:4-5, NKJV).

Every night I would rub lotion on my belly—it was actually a concoction of cheap lotion and hair grease that I was able to purchase through the commissary. I would rub it on my growing belly, and we would read our verses out loud and pray over Noah. Looking back, I can see we were literally anointing Noah in the womb. Lindy would rest her head on my baby bump and talk to Noah every single day and night. I treasure those moments. Even out of such a dark and seemingly hopeless situation, God filled me with joy and love. This is my beauty from ashes.

LINDY'S PERSPECTIVE

I can remember the day that I found out my sister was pregnant. In the midst of all that darkness and chaos, the thought of having a baby in our family somehow brought me so much hope. He was a light in our dark world, long before he even took his first breath.

We proclaimed that Christ would always be at the center of his life, and that is a truth that we all still stand on today.

Being incarcerated is one of the loneliest, most hopeless things that a person could ever go through. My unborn nephew brought us so much joy there. Just thinking about that time in our lives, when we would sit and talk about him and daydream about what he would be like, brings a smile to my face even now. The thought of that precious baby boy gave us so much motivation to keep going because better things were in store for us all.

We used to pray over that baby boy day and night while he was still in my sister's womb. We prayed over his life and the man of God that we knew he would grow up to be. We both had scripture verses that we would speak and declare over Noah's life as we would lay hands on Eden's belly. We knew the power of life that we held in our words, and we chose to stand firm in our faith that the Lord would be faithful to His word and fulfill His promises to us concerning our precious little baby.

I remember sitting in our jail cell talking about boy names with Eden. She said that she wanted to name him Noah. We both loved that name so much and could not wait to hold our sweet baby, Noah. She let me choose his middle name and I chose Christopher. I chose the name Christopher in memory of my uncle who had passed away when I was a child. He was a great man who loved and served the Lord with all of his heart, and his legacy will live on through Noah Christopher. This baby was our miracle, and he would forever change all of our lives. We proclaimed that Christ would always be at the center of his life, and that is a truth that we all still stand on today.

CHAPTER 11

Forgiveness and the Tattoo

*Get rid of all bitterness, rage and anger, brawling
and slander, along with every form of malice. Be
kind and compassionate to one another, forgiving
each other, just as in Christ God forgave you.*
—EPHESIANS 4:31-32

THE TEN COMMANDMENTS

Before mercy and grace came through Jesus, we had the law—the Ten Commandments of which we could never keep and never obey.

A friend of mine posted this question on Facebook one day, "Have any of you ever broken all ten commandments?"

1) Do not have any other gods before God.

2) Do not make yourself an idol.

3) Do not take the Lord's name in vain.

4) Remember the Sabbath Day and keep it holy.

5) Honor thy mother and father.

6) Do not murder.

7) Do not commit adultery.

8) Do not steal.

9) Do not bear false witness against your neighbor.

10) Do not covet.

I messaged her back with this statement "Yes, I have."

She then sends me a private message and asks, "Is there something you need to tell me?"

I replied, "What do you mean?" She said, "Like did you kill somebody?"

I sent this message back, "I have hated" and it says in, 1 John 3:15, "Whoever hates his brother is a murderer . . ." (1 John 3:15, NKJV). So that makes me a murderer.

We need to recognize that we are all

sinners in need of a Savior.

She messaged back these words, "Oh . . . ok." I could sense the sigh of relief. I could almost hear the "whew" coming through the computer, as if to say "That's ok . . . thank God. This is a good friend of mine; I know her well and knew this wasn't what she really meant. But sadly, that's how we often think. It's okay if you hate as long as you don't kill. It's okay if you gossip as long as you don't lie. It's okay if you _____ as long as you don't _____. You just fill in the blank.

God's word says in James, "For whoever keeps the whole law and yet stumbles at just ONE is guilty of breaking ALL of it" (James 2:10, author emphasis).

We could not obey the law. Sin separated us from God, and we all needed a solution. His name is Jesus.

We need to recognize that we are all sinners in need of a Savior. "For the wages of sin is death, but the gift of God is eternal life in Christ Jesus our Lord" (Romans 6:23). We all have a debt we cannot pay, but Jesus paid it all on the cross of calvary. "There is no one righteous, not even one" (Romans 3:10).

UNFORGIVENESS

I had hatred and unforgiveness in my heart for Donnie, even though I knew the prison of unforgiveness from past experiences in my life. I knew what unforgiveness would do to me, my family, and my relationship with the Lord, but I couldn't seem to let it go and give it to Jesus.

John Wesley says, "Unforgiveness is like drinking poison and expecting the other person to die."[5]

---

5   https://bibleteachinglady.com/

I by no means thought of Eden as innocent. She definitely had made her own choices. In reality, it was easier for me to blame Donnie than my own daughter. Part of what I could not let go of was the fact he was so much older than her by almost twenty years. I couldn't stop thinking, *didn't he know better?* What was an almost forty-year-old man doing out with these young girls cooking dope and committing crimes? Now, here my daughter was twenty years old facing felony charges for manufacturing drugs, not to mention the possibility of my grandson growing up without a mom or a dad, because both would be incarcerated if convicted.

The more I thought about it, the deeper my anger grew. I'm not saying these thoughts or feelings were right; I'm just being transparent. Transparent is God's favorite color. I'm merely trying to be honest and tell my story and more importantly how Jesus can and will change everything. Even my old bitter heart.

The Bible says, "See to it that no one falls short of the grace of God and that no bitter root grows up to cause trouble and defile many" (Hebrews 12:15).

I was definitely falling short of showing God's grace. Here's the sad thing about bitter roots. It is not only you that it's hurting. Notice those two little words at the end of that verse: "defile many." You won't be the only one affected by your bitterness, which I call unforgiveness on steroids. Sadly, it will affect your relationship with the Lord, your kids, your marriage, your family, your friendships, your job, your rest/sleep, your health—every part of your life. It will ultimately rob you of your peace and joy. It's like the ripple effect of throwing a stone in a lake.

The Bible says that we were by nature deserving of wrath. But because of his great love for us, God, who is rich in mercy, made us alive with Christ even when we were dead in our sin—it is by grace you have been saved" (Ephesians 2:3-5, author paraphrase).

I had taught my children about forgiveness and made sure they were in church every Sunday to learn more about forgiveness. But now it was up to me to demonstrate it, to live it. What better way to teach it to your children than to show them how it's done? This was not easy!

You can't give something away that
you do not have yourself.

The simple definition of Grace is the unearned, unmerited favor of God. . . . but it's oh so much more. Grace is like *Super-califragilisticexpialidocious.* Have you ever looked that word up? It implies all that is grand, great, glorious, splendid, superb, and wonderful. Grace is all of that and then some. We can't earn it and we don't deserve it.

Grace is a free gift. What has to happen for a gift to be of any value? It has to be received, opened, and used.

Like that wrinkle cream on your nightstand—it ain't gonna do you a bit of good if you don't open that bottle up and use it.

Mercy and grace are like cousins. I heard it put this way: Mercy is God not giving us what we do deserve, which is judgment;

Grace is God giving us what we do not deserve, which is mercy and forgiveness.

Here's the deal. You can't give something away that you do not have yourself. I can't give you $10 if the balance in my account is zero. If you have never opened your heart and received God's forgiveness and Grace, then you can't possibly give it away. On the other hand, if you have received it, then it's time to get a hold of what Jesus has done for you and pay it forward. Who are we to withhold forgiveness and grace after all the forgiveness and Grace Jesus has lavished on us when we didn't even deserve it? I find that we want to use an eighth of a teaspoon when we need to give forgiveness but when we are in need of receiving forgiveness, we want—and even expect it—by the bucket full.

Jesus said, "For if you forgive other people when they sin against you, your heavenly Father will also forgive you. But if you do not forgive others their sins, your Father will not forgive your sins" (Matthew 6:14-15).

Woo-wee! That's a debt I cannot afford!

FORGIVENESS AND THE LETTER

One day, when my mind was replaying all those hate records, God interrupted those thought waves with an important announcement. The Lord talks to me like I talk to my kids sometimes, saying, "Who do you think you are, little girl?" I sensed the Lord saying, "Lori, I love Donnie just as much as I love you. I died on the cross and shed my blood for him just like I did for you." My heart was broken. I knew at that moment I needed to love and forgive him, even pray for him, but how? I felt like I couldn't.

I thought back to a few things my Dad had told me years earlier, "Forgiveness is a choice, not a feeling." "Your emotions need to follow your choices, not your choices follow your emotions." "Your feelings will mislead you." He would say, "Just choose to forgive and out of that obedience your feelings will follow."

God doesn't expect that we will have it all figured out. He understands we're limited, that's why we need Him to make us limitless in pouring out His love, mercy, grace, and forgiveness. So, I began to pray for myself the same thing I had prayed for my kids, by changing my "want to". "Lord, I don't want to love or forgive Donnie, please change my "want to". If you pray for God to change your "want to," you better expect something is gonna happen.

First of all, I want to say that I believe forgiveness is one of the hardest things that you will ever have to wrestle with in life. The forgiveness that I needed to give started as a process through what I call conviction. It's like the Holy Spirit nagging, sort of pulling at your heart, and honestly, we want to ignore it. First of all, I began to search for scriptures about forgiveness—and there are a lot of them. There were verses that talked about how if I don't forgive others, Jesus won't forgive me and how can I say I love Jesus if I hate my brother? Also, the thought of bitterness affecting "many" was not something that I wanted in my life. I began to reflect on all the forgiveness I had received in my life for all the wrongs and all the sins that I was guilty of. I knew about forgiveness and what I had been taught. I started trying to consider Donnie, thinking that maybe he had been through some hard things in his life. I began to ask the Lord to put the love in my heart for Donnie that I did not have and to help me forgive him. God did just that; He is faithful to His word. When our prayers line up with His will . . . He will provide. If we are willing, God is certainly able. This reminds me of the story of the paralyzed man in John 5:6 where Jesus walks up to him and says, "Do you want to get well?" That seemed so odd to me; what crippled person wouldn't want to walk!! The truth is we all have situations that we're in that have us crippled and we need to ask ourselves that same question, "Do I want to get well?" Some people are addicted to pain, drama, and feeling sorry for themselves. Pain can become your idol. Forgiveness does not mean that we don't validate and acknowledge what happened and it doesn't mean we're saying what was done is okay because it's not. Forgiveness frees you from those chains of imprisonment. Even freeing the guilty party. Forgiveness is not about the other person deserving it. God forgave us when we did not deserve it. It's letting God be Judge, because truly, that position belongs to Him. God put a love and forgiveness in my heart for Donnie that I didn't think was possible. I began to even pray for him.

Donnie was convicted of the murder of a fellow gang member and was sentenced to life in prison. There are several newspaper articles giving details of this story. There seems to be evidence that there were two shooters, but to our knowledge, no one else has been charged.

I sensed the Holy Spirit telling me to write him a letter. So I did. I wrote him a short letter in prison telling him "Jesus loves you this I know, for the Bible tells me so." He sent me back a letter and bookmark that had John 3:16 on it. To this day I pray for him and his mama. My heart breaks for her; no matter what, he is her son, and she loves him.

We all have a story that sometimes leads us to make wrong decisions. The truth is, we all need Jesus. We all need His forgiveness. How will anyone see Jesus unless it's through us, the ones who claim to know Him?

THE TATTOO

Around April 2011, Eden and Lindy were still in jail. So, I took a trip to Minnesota to visit my daughter Kristin. I told her I wanted to get a tattoo. This was a huge decision. I had never liked tattoos and to be honest would sit in judgment when I would see a person with tattoos, even though three of my daughters had them. It was time to stop judging and start loving. I wanted something to remind me of what the Lord had told me about Donnie—that He loves him and shed his blood for him just like He did for me. Jesus' love and forgiveness are for everyone, and I wanted a forever reminder.

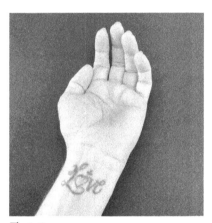

The tattoo

I found the one I wanted. Kristin proudly drove me to the tattoo shop, even though she is my only daughter that does not have a tattoo. The tattoo artist was a no-nonsense kind of guy; nonetheless, I felt the need to tell him a little of the story behind my tattoo and the journey I was on. Clearly, he did not share my beliefs, hence the opportunity to show the love of Jesus started right in the middle of getting the "Love" tattoo. Of course. Isn't that how Jesus works?

I shared with him the story of my own hate and unforgiveness and how I had needed a heart change. I explained to him how I was reminded that Jesus loves everyone and shed His blood on the cross for all of us. The tattoo artist replied, in somewhat of a monotone voice, "That's religious," not in a condescending way, but more like a matter-of-fact way. I replied, "Actually, Jesus hates religion and that's a lot of what's wrong with our world today." Jesus didn't give His life for religion; He gave His life for relationship. Jesus wants to have a personal relationship with us.

As I left that day, I thanked him for the tattoo and told him how much I liked it. I also told him Jesus loves him. I pray that somehow a seed was planted that would help him come to know the love of Jesus. Now I'm trying to decide what tattoo I need next. I pray that the next one doesn't come from a place of adversity!!

CHAPTER 12

ATW

. . . He has sent me to bind up the brokenhearted,
to proclaim freedom for the captives and release
from darkness for the prisoners . . .
—Isaiah 61:1

BAIL

Papoo and Eden had a close relationship. She contacted him after staying a while in jail to ask him to consider helping her get out by posting her bond.

You are probably wondering and maybe even disagree as to why I didn't post bond for my pregnant daughter to get out of jail. I had a very hard decision to make. Through a lot of prayer, I made a decision to trust God and leave her in jail. I did not feel that it was the right thing to run down there and get her out to go right back to drugs and the streets. There are consequences for our decisions, and how was she ever going to learn this and change her life as long as I kept running interference? She had refused to heed any of my advice to prevent her from ending up here and had no regard for me. I truly felt that if I bonded her out, it would mean nothing for her to skip bail, putting her life and her baby's life right back in danger.

God is not always about the easy way out, but I

know this for sure—His way is the best way.

These were serious charges, and I felt it was time for her to figure some things out. She needed some sober time to do this. Sometimes we interfere with God's plans and what he wants to do with our kids because we're too busy doing what we want to do—advancing our plan. Sometimes we don't stop long enough to hear what God is saying and sometimes we just outright disobey Him because we don't want to do what we know He wants, because maybe it's the hard way. God is not always about the easy way out, but I know this for sure—His way is the best way. Isaiah tells us that God's ways are higher than our ways and His thoughts are higher than our thoughts. Trust God's way. These may be merely words on a piece of paper to some of you, but this was my life, and these were gut-wrenching decisions. Addiction had a stronghold on Eden; her life and the life of her baby were at stake. She had been telling all of us that she was not going to stay a day past June 30th in jail. I asked her how she knew this, and she said "I don't know how, but I just know." She had no facts to base this on but had spent a lot of time praying, and it was just a feeling she had inside—actually, it was more than a feeling— somehow Eden knew it as a truth. So, who was I to disagree? I stood in agreement with her because I definitely wanted her to come home too. By now she had turned her life back over to Jesus and was back to being the daughter I knew before drugs. When someone is addicted to drugs, you no longer have a relationship with them; it is no longer the person you know and love because the relationship becomes all about the drugs. I was so excited that I was going to get to spend some sober time with Eden.

The day had arrived, June 30th, but there was no plan for release until the phone rang that morning, and Papoo said he was posting bond. He did not actually come to Mobile; he just sent the money for the bond because Eden had called him a few days before to ask for his help, but she didn't hear back from him, so she didn't know if he was going to help her out. I could not believe it. He called on the exact date that she said she was getting out.

I had never gotten anyone out of jail before and did not have a clue what to do. So, I asked around and I called a bail bondsman who was right by the Mobile Metro Jail to find out what I needed to do. Can I just tell you; I never felt safe driving anywhere near this jail. It is pretty much a run-down, slum area. But on this day, I rushed down there, ready to see my girl with no worries.

I pulled up to that ragged old bail bondsman's trailer, got out of the car, and walked up to the door. I waited inside for her to be released and meet me there. It seemed like an eternity, but when I heard that door handle turn, that door opened and there she stood—no chains, no bars, no glass window, no blue jump-suit—she was clothed and in her right mind. The prodigal had come home. The minute we saw each other, we started screaming, crying, and laughing all at the same time. As we jumped up and down, we "squeezed" each other for the first time in a long time. She lifted her shirt up to show me how big her belly was. We laughed so hard at how it was sticking out of her jeans; she couldn't even get them zipped.

After serving a little over three months in jail, the day had come just as Eden said it would. The paperwork was stamped June 30th, 2011! What a celebration!! Sadly, Lindy had to stay. She had been arrested many times before and this time she served almost a year before she was released.

EDEN'S PERSPECTIVE

I made a phone call to my Papoo around June 23rd to ask him if he would bail me out, but I had not heard back from him. June 30th came and that morning, I was sitting in my cell, waiting, wondering what happened, because this was the release date I had been believing for and claiming. All of a sudden, I heard over the intercom, "Elizabeth Metzger ATW," which means "at the window". This was music to my ears, because any inmate knew that ATW meant someone is bonding you out! I jumped up and gave all of my stuff away to other inmates. I knew they would need it more than me because now I would be home and have everything I needed—and a whole lot of what I wanted. I had no idea that Papoo had called my mom to make arrangements to pay my bail. I was so thankful and so excited!

Once bail is posted, the guard takes the inmate to the discharge area to return the belongings they came in with. The inmate then has to change back into those same clothes. Well, there was a little problem. I was now five months pregnant and that belly was not going back into those jeans. I didn't care, I pulled and wiggled and got those jeans back on. They were so tight I could not get them zipped. My pants were gaping wide open with my belly sticking out in between. I was able to pull my shirt over my belly and was ready to go.

There are several bond companies around the jail. They told me which "bondsman's trailer" had posted the bond. It was only a few blocks away and I walked there—more like a speed walk. I was so excited. This was the day I had been praying and waiting for.

CHAPTER 13

Life While Waiting on My Day in Court

A merry heart doeth good like a medicine. . . .
—Proverbs 17:22 (KJV)

GETTING THE NURSERY READY

Shortly after Eden was released from jail, we scheduled a 3-D ultrasound. We were told, "It's a boy!!" Eden already knew this in her heart and was not surprised. Have you ever seen a 3-D ultrasound? Let's be real, the babies look like aliens, but somehow, we thought Noah was beautiful in his 3-D photo shoot. Lord help us. Now that we knew for sure she was having a boy there was nothing left to do but get that nursery room ready and buy all the boy clothes that the closet could hold.

We found a good deal on a baby bed with a changing table and added the baby comfort set. Now all we needed was the baby. Eden chose animals for his room decor. It sort of went along with the name Noah. We had a fun baby shower, where she received lots of love and great gifts from friends and family. Kristin had bought some wooden letters that spelled out N-O-A-H. She painted them to match his room. Eden hung them on the wall. On the dresser, she put a picture frame with the Bible verse that God had given to her about Noah while in jail. "I will make you into a great nation and I will bless you. I will make your name great and you will be a blessing. I will bless those who bless you and whoever curses you I will curse. And all peoples on Earth will be blessed through you" (Genesis 12:2-3).

She prayed this scripture over him every day until the day he arrived. We were overjoyed. What was I going to do with a little boy? All I had ever known was beauties and bows because I had four daughters.

In just a few short months, I would find out what I was going to do—love him to the moon and back!!

Eden's appetite was like a bottomless pit. Seemed like we couldn't keep her filled up. So happy she was home and eating well, we gladly took her to Waffle House or Bama Belle almost every morning. Bama Belle had it going on with their southern cooking. They had this breakfast plate that was literally piled about six inches high with scrambled eggs, sausage, sausage gravy, and hash browns, and she would eat the whole thing. No wonder Noah weighed almost eight pounds at birth.

OBGYN VISITS TOGETHER

Eden really liked her OBGYN doctor that was appointed to her while she was in jail. So, after she was released, she decided to continue under her care. She said she felt a connection with her. She was a good, down-to-earth doctor. Perfect for us during this difficult time. She did not look down on Eden but treated her with kindness and respect.

Dr. D. said she witnessed the transformation in Eden's life first-hand, from the first visit of an angry, scared, pregnant inmate to this happy, fearless, free girl. She told us she had never been privileged to see a story like Eden's.

Usually, she said, when she cared for incarcerated pregnant patients, she wouldn't get to see them again once they had been released. She told us how happy she was that Eden chose to continue under her care. God was already working on using this story for His glory.

The most exciting part for us was that I could now go to all the doctor visits with Eden—no shackles and no guards. One day during an office visit when they had left us in the examining room, we were getting bored. No worries, we knew how to entertain ourselves. We started cracking ourselves up, as usual. Eden was sitting on this little stool in the room that the doctor usually sits on, and she had taken the folded sheet and put it over her head like Mary, the mother of Jesus. As we were sitting there talking, she started singing the song "Mary, Did You Know"? We were laughing so hard and loud that the nurse came rushing in to see about us. She thought we were crying. Laughing is our favorite thing to do, and we're good at it. We do it often.

Dr. D. moved shortly after delivering Noah, but she and Eden stayed in contact on Facebook.

LET ME GET MY WHITES ON

A couple of months after Eden was released from jail, we were at our house upstairs just hanging out when we heard the doorbell ring. We weren't expecting anyone, so we looked out of the upstairs window. Oh no, a police car was parked in front of our house. Our hearts begin to pound. You have to understand with all we had been through, the sight of a police officer at our house was definitely unsettling. We couldn't imagine what in the world an officer would be doing at our house.

Eden began to panic and said, "I don't know why, but I must be getting arrested again. Mom let me get my whites on." I said, "What?" She said, "Just go downstairs and try to stall them for just a few minutes and I'll be right there after I get dressed." We were so upset. My heart was pounding as I slowly walked down those stairs trying to figure out what in the world I was going to say in order to "stall" a police officer. I opened the door and the officer said, "We're looking for a Mr. Jones, is he here?" At this point I could barely speak, I said, "No . . . no sir, I don't know Mr. Jones, there's no one here by that name." He said, "ok thank you, have a nice day" and just like that, he left. I thought . . . Have a nice day?—I was about to have a heart attack!! Just as I was closing the door, I looked up, and here comes Eden walking down the stairs with her whites on, dressed for jail. I looked at her and said, "He was looking for Mr. Jones. After all that panicking, he wasn't even looking for you." We belly laughed so hard tears were rolling down our cheeks. Tears of laughter as well as relief. Let me explain the "whites". When you get arrested and put in jail, you are only allowed to wear a white bra, white underwear, and a white T-shirt under the jumpsuit that they give you while incarcerated. If you didn't come in wearing whites, then you were out of luck unless your family put money on your books to purchase a set from the jail commissary. When Eden was first arrested back in March, I put money on her "books" so that she could purchase a set of "whites". Their "whites" must be some "high cotton" because they're not cheap. Eden figured that if she was going to jail again, this time she was going to be prepared—wearing whites.

EDEN'S PERSPECTIVE

After my release, my Mom became my best friend. I was so determined not to go back to drugs and the life I had left behind. I rarely went anywhere without my Mom, because I knew she was a safe person for me and supported me in my commitment to my sobriety.

I realized how important it is to reach our teens and

how easy it is to lose them to all kinds of rebellion.

A lot of hard days lay ahead of us. We didn't know what would happen with my court dates yet to come. Despite those uncertainties, one of the first things I did was go back to church. It had definitely been a while since I had been there and desired to be in Christian fellowship. Some of our close friends had started this church, and I got very involved in helping with the youth. Those close friends knew my Mom and had known me all of my life. They took me right in and allowed me to pour life into those teens after my release from jail. I realized how important it is to reach our teens and how easy it is to lose them to all kinds of rebellion. So, who better to sow into the lives of teenagers than me? Somebody who had been there. I had been there and done that and didn't even get a T-shirt. Well, maybe a white one.

CHAPTER 14

Day of Sentencing

. . . The effectual fervent prayer of a righteous man availeth much.
—James 5:16 (KJV)

PRAYERS THAT AVAIL MUCH

Several months before Eden's trial for charges of manufacturing meth, we went to meet with our attorney, Michael Newton. He loves Jesus and believes in the power of prayer. As we were sitting in his office that day discussing the case, he reached down and pulled out a little book called *Prayers That Avail Much* by Germaine Copeland. He turned in the book to a prayer titled "In Court Cases" and read it to us:

> *Father, in the name of Jesus, it is written in Your Word to call on You and You will answer me and show me great and*

mighty things. I put You in remembrance of Your Word and thank You that You watch over it to perform it.

I say that no weapon formed against me shall prosper, and any tongue that rises against me in judgment I shall show to be in the wrong. This peace, security, and triumph over opposition is my inheritance as Your child. This is the righteousness I obtain from You, Father, which You impart to me as my justification. I am far from even the thought of destruction; for I shall not fear, and terror shall not come near me.

Father, You say You will establish me to the end—keep me steadfast, give me strength, and guarantee my vindication; That is, be my warrant against all accusations or indictment. Father, You contend with those who contend with me, and You perfect that which concerns me. I dwell in the secret place of the Most High, and this secret place hides me from the strife of tongues, for a false witness who breathes out lies is an abomination to You.

I am a true witness, and all my words are upright and in right standing with You, Father. By my long forbearing and calmness of spirit the judge is persuaded, and my soft speech breaks down the most bone-like resistance. Therefore, I am not anxious beforehand how I shall reply in defense or what I am to say, for the Holy Spirit teaches me in that very hour and moment what I ought to say to those in the outside world. My speech is seasoned with salt.

As a child of light, I enforce the triumphant victory of my Lord Jesus Christ in this situation, knowing that all of Heaven is backing me. I am strong in You, Lord, and in the power of Your might. Thank You for the shield of faith that quenches every fiery dart of the enemy. I am increasing in wisdom and in stature and in years, and in favor with You, Father, and with man. Praise the Lord! Amen.[6]

---

6   Germaine Copeland, "In Court Cases," *Prayers That Avail Much* (Harrison House, 2005), p. 221-222.

Our attorney told us that he wanted all of us to start praying this prayer over Eden, to be in agreement and believe for God to move. We got right on it. We bought the book and began earnestly praying that prayer.

EDEN'S DAY IN COURT

Around October 2011, at eight months pregnant, Eden's day in court had finally arrived. The case would be presented to Judge W., and he would be handing down the sentence.

The original charge carried a 30-year prison sentence. We needed a miracle, but we knew God had done it before and could do it again. We had a large group of people there that day to support Eden and pray. Even though we were nervous entering the courtroom, Eden and I had agreed in prayer that God was going to intervene on her behalf and that she would raise her son.

It was 9:00 a.m. and court was now in session. Desperation has a sound. The sound of the judge's mallet striking the podium as court was called to order knowing your daughter's life was in his hands. We were storming heaven with our prayers because I knew that ultimately her life was in God's hands. Although the trafficking charges had been dropped, she was still facing twenty years for felony manufacturing of drugs.

I don't remember everyone who was with us, but I do remember it was Mamaw, Papaw, our pastors, the youth pastor Eden was doing volunteer work with, and several other friends for support. Judge W. called a few of our friends up one at a time to the front as character witnesses. He then called me. I had no idea I would be able to speak on behalf of my daughter on this day. I prayed,

"Lord give me wisdom, give me words," as I made my way to the front of the courtroom.

Judge W. was actually kind. He asked me a few questions, basically about our family dynamics . . . Mom, Dad, etc. I explained her Dad had passed in 2007, and it was just me. He then asked me to tell him about Eden. I began to tell him how she had been raised in the church and gave her heart to Jesus at a young age. She was a good leader, good student, and had been a great daughter up to this point. She had traveled down a road of rebellion and began running with the wrong people, making bad choices, and had lost her way, and that is what has brought us here. I also explained to him that I truly believe that she had changed. She had turned her life back to Jesus and was now living with me and sharing her story with the youth at the church where she was volunteering.

After the judge was finished with all the witnesses, Eden and I were taken to a little room just outside the courtroom for a private meeting with our attorney. We stood there and prayed for God's favor and guidance.

So let me explain; the purpose of the court hearing that day was for the D.A. to make an offer to Eden; she could accept the offer from the D.A., and the judge would then rule or reject the offer and go to trial.

The first offer from the D.A. was five years in prison. Eden said no.

It was scary but we had made a decision to believe God for no prison time. The D.A. came back with a three-year offer and Eden said no, again.

A few minutes later the D.A. came in and offered her one year in prison. He stepped out for a minute while we talked with her attorney. Our attorney advised her to take the deal that the D.A.

had offered, and any good attorney would have advised her to take this offer. She turned it down and told him no, and again I agreed, even though our hearts were pounding.

Our attorney advised her again, saying, "Eden, you need to take this offer, we've come a long way from twenty years down to one year. If we go to trial, you could end up getting a lot more time; this is a good offer; take it." He said, "Your Mom can keep the baby and you'll be out in a year." Eden replied, "No, I'm believing God that I'm not going to spend one day in prison. I'm going to raise my baby."

The D.A. came back, and our attorney reluctantly said no to the one-year offer. He then said, "Let me go make a phone call and I'll be right back." He leaves. We pray. He came back and said, "I didn't come here today expecting to see what I am seeing—the change in Eden." He then offered a sentence of three years of probation with no time in prison unless she got in trouble during those three years, but if she did, then she would go to prison and serve her time. Tears of joy and praise filled that room as we all cried and embraced. We witnessed a miracle!

_____

God entered that courtroom on Eden's behalf and moved the hand of the D.A. and Judge in her favor.

_____

We were then led back into the courtroom and Eden again stood before the judge. The D.A. made their recommendation,

"Front end diversion of twenty-split-three to serve one year in prison." Judge W. said, "In all my years of serving as a judge I have never done a reverse sentence like this." He told the court reporter to be sure and write it down correctly and repeated it to her several times. He said, "I'm retiring next year, and I don't want you to have to come looking for me if this gets messed up."

Normally, you serve your prison time first and then your probation. But in Eden's case, they were giving her probation first, and if she violated probation during those three years, she would be taken to prison to serve her time. We witnessed a miracle that day. God entered that courtroom on Eden's behalf and moved the hand of the D.A. and Judge in her favor. He allowed her to go free with probation. She was going to be able to raise her son.

She was never implicated in the murder and had no part in it.

Eden was then assigned to a probation officer that she would be meeting with over the next three years, drug testing on a regular basis.

POWER OF PRAYER

Through all these prayers, we saw the favor and hand of God move over Eden's life in the courtroom that day. Our attorney has since then asked several families to pray that same prayer over their situation, using Eden's story as an example while maintaining her anonymity.

Germaine Copeland, the author of the prayer book, held a conference in Mobile in 2018, and our Attorney Michel Newton attended. Through a chain of events, he was able to meet Mrs. Copeland during the break at this conference. After the break, he had the honor of being called to the platform to tell what this book meant to him. He gave a short testimony of Eden's story and how God used one of the prayers to help change the course of one young girl's life whom he had represented and how he has used it as a tool to witness and pray with many of his clients.

EDEN'S PERSPECTIVE

I was very nervous going into the courtroom on this day. We had a lot of people praying, and Mom and I were standing in agreement that I would not have to serve even one day in prison, and that I would get to raise my son. But there were no guarantees. Deliverance does not always come in the way that we want or even pray. Sometimes we still have to pay the consequences of our decisions, but I was still going to ask God for a miracle. We stood there in faith turning down every offer from the D.A. that involved prison time. Then came the final offer of "three years of probation with no time in prison." As my mom already explained, the D.A. offered a twenty-split-three to serve one year in prison on a front-end diversion—and that meant I would not be going to jail! Mom and I shouted, "Thank you Jesus!" as we stood there hugging while crying tears of relief and joy. Our attorney joined in.

CHAPTER 15

Honey from the Rock

> *". . . With honey from the rock I would satisfy you."*
> —Psalm 81:16

LABOR AND DELIVERY

*E*den was thirty-eight weeks pregnant, and we were going for weekly visits now. Dr. D. told us that she was going on vacation the week that Noah was due and that she wanted to be the one to deliver him. She said to Eden, "I want to do a maneuver to possibly help you go into labor on your own, but just in case that doesn't work, I want to go ahead and get you scheduled for an induction." They both agreed and that's what was done. Dr. D.

did the procedure and scheduled the induction for November 8th, 2011. It seemed like time stood still after that; we waited every day, but no labor. We were packed and ready. Sitting on "G" waiting on "O" . . . Go time!!

Then came the BIG DAY, November 8th, when Eden was going to be induced. It was a Tuesday morning. I woke up early and was doing some Bible reading when Eden came into the living room to tell me that she "had a dream that we were in a store walking around and she was bent over in pain holding her stomach." She went on to say that the actual pain woke her up from her dream and that she was in labor. I jumped up and we immediately started timing the contractions. They were not very close together, so we calmed down and thought, *Oh well, we have time.* We got our showers and took our time getting ready with no sense of urgency, but still timing the contractions.

After we were finally dressed and ready, the contractions began to get more intense and closer together. We loaded up the car and headed to the hospital. But that girl was gonna eat no matter what. Eden said, "Mom, it's gonna be a while before I get to eat so I'm gonna need some breakfast." So of course, the first stop was a drive-thru. I have to say she comes by it honestly, though. When my family would go on a trip, the first stop my Dad would make was to get food, sometimes before we even got out of our hometown. So, it's passed on to generations.

We made it to the hospital and the contractions were very intense. If you know Eden, she can't stand getting her blood drawn or IVs; she passes out almost every time, but those contractions were so painful, she was like, "Bring it on, I need relief!"

They got the IV started, gave her something for pain, and hooked her up to all the monitors to record the contractions and the baby's heartbeat. She was dilating well, so they gave her the epidural and broke her water. Now it was just a matter of time.

A friend of Eden's drove her sister, Mary Kathryn, to the hospital so that she could be there for the birth. This friend also wanted to be there for her and visit a bit before the baby came. The Children's Pastor from our church came to visit and pray with us before Noah was born. We were sitting there chatting when all of a sudden Eden said, "I feel a lot of pressure, tell the nurse I need the bedpan." She said, "I think he's coming!" I pushed

the button for the nurse. The pastor stood up and was out of there. I think his job was baptizing babies, not delivering them! Everyone left, so only me and Mary Kathryn were there to help Eden welcome Noah into this world.

Nurses rushed in and began getting everything ready. We couldn't under-

Baby Noah

stand why she was feeling so much of the pain. The doctor came in and explained to us that her epidural was occluded, meaning the epidural tube was clogged up, and that it was too late to fix it because it was pushing time.

I was on one side holding Eden's leg and Mary Kathryn was holding the other leg. We would help push her legs to her chest as the doctor instructed Eden to take a deep breath and push. After the third round of this pushing, Noah was born. Tears of joy flowed down our cheeks. There he was, now lying on his mama's chest.

He was the honey from that rock, the sweetest thing that God brought out of the hardest place of my life.

Of course, I got a hold of him just as soon as I could. When I held that little precious angel in my arms, overwhelming tears of joy flooded my face. I was in love, pure love.

Mary Kathryn got her turn, and with tears running down her smiling cheeks, she held the one who made her an aunt. She was in love.

To this day, she is called "YaYa" because Noah could not say Mary Kathryn.

My heart was forever his. I was thankful to God that Noah was alive and well. There were no side effects from the drugs. He was perfect in every way. My first grandbaby!

He was the honey from that rock, the sweetest thing that God brought out of the hardest place of my life.

All of those thoughts of not being ready to be a grandmom were nowhere to be found!! GG was his, and he was mine!

THE PERFECT PEDIATRICIAN

I don't know why, but we had not chosen a pediatrician. We had one assigned to us to follow up with after leaving the hospital. Shortly after he was born, we went for a doctor's visit.

The doctor was foreign with a strong accent. Of course, me being the Bama redneck that I am, could not understand half of what he was saying. I don't think he could understand me either. Even though we were both speaking English, I felt like we needed an interpreter. The doctor left the room, and I began to pray under my breath, "Lord, help, Lord help, Lord help." Somehow, I felt the Lord was secretly getting a laugh out of this. . . . oh you don't think God laughs? Uh, you need to just look around and listen. Or follow me around for a day. I said, "Eden, what are we going to do? I don't want to be rude, but I literally cannot understand him." It was at about that time the nurse came in and I said, "I'm so sorry and I'm not trying to be disrespectful, but can y'all please get someone in here that we can understand? Ma'am, I can't understand his accent. It's important that we understand what he is saying." My thought was, *My accent is so strong, even Siri can't understand me*. No matter what I ask Siri, she repeats something totally different back to me—so frustrating. I was feeling some of that frustration and I said to the nurse, "Please, can you help us?"

That's when we met the greatest pediatrician in the world, Dr. C., head of Pediatrics at Women's and Children. She took over Noah's care. She seemed to understand me and love my grandbaby. What more could I want? Thank you, Lord.

BABY DEDICATION

When Noah was about seven months old, we dedicated him to the Lord on our back porch. We invited a few of our friends over to lay hands on him and pray as my Dad dedicated him to the Lord. It was such a special moment. In fact, some of the people there that day were the very ones whom I had texted to pray for Eden when she was missing and I could not find her. These people are my brothers and sisters in Christ. Truly God-fearing prayer warriors.

Noah's dedication

NOAH STORIES

The way I figure, there's no room for rebellion in Noah's life. Before he was even born, he had consumed cigarettes, drugs, alcohol, and had already been to jail. He has an awesome testimony, good to go, ready to serve the Lord. I do pray that he will love and serve the Lord all the days of his life. I pray for not one day of rebellion.

Noah jumping

Noah is wild at heart, rambunctious, smart, funny, loving, and kind. He loves music, swimming, the beach, video games, and jumping on anything—a trampoline, my bed, my couch, or just standing there jumping up and down. Rocking with his GG and playing in the rain are two of his favorite things. When he was little, he couldn't say rain; he called it "wain."

To this day, Noah and I say to each other, "I love you to the moon and back," but he added, "GG, I love you to the moon and back, the stars and back, and to heaven and back." One day when he was trying to think of the most awesome way he could express his love to me, he added, "to the Holy Spirit and back." I guess to him the Holy Spirit was the biggest, most awesome thing he could think of—I love it!!

Noah was born to worship. There's one day I'll never forget. When he was about two and a half years old, we were home, and I was upstairs putting on makeup. He ran into the bathroom and said, "Come on, GG." I said, "What is it?" He grabbed my hand and started pulling me into the other bedroom where we had worship music playing. He wanted me to come worship with him. Just as we entered the room, he threw his little arms in the air as he stood there dressed in just a diaper with his arms raised in praise literally for several minutes. I raised my hands, too, with a heart overflowing with gratitude for this precious little boy. His love for Jesus was contagious.

One night, when he was around four years old, we took him to a Big Daddy Weave concert at a football stadium. He got down out of the bleachers and began to dance on the concrete walkway. I mean—he cut loose—even spinning around on the ground like he knew how to breakdance. He was in his own world, just like he and Jesus were the only two at that concert. It was awesome.

Later on that night, these people came and sat in front of us, eating nachos and cheese. Noah said, "I smell sumpin'. . . . it smells like puppies but it's not." We busted out laughing. He was quite the entertainer, just like his mom.

Noah and my Dad, who was his great-granddad, were best buds. My Dad had an electric shaver, and every morning he and Noah would shave, put on cologne, and comb their hair. A precious memory. One day, when Noah was around the age of two, my dad was very sick in bed. Noah walked into his room, stood at the end of his bed, stretched out his little hand toward my dad, and said, "Heal, heal, heal." I just stood there amazed. Actually, my dad did recover and lived another two months. But oh, how I wish we as Christians could have the boldness of that two-year-old!!

My Mom and Noah were nearly inseparable. We all lived together the first three years of his life. He and my Mom had a weekly routine of going to Dollar General. He couldn't say it, so for him, it was "Darlar Gentral," but he knew his Mamaw was going to buy him whatever he wanted.

When Noah was four years old, we were attending the wedding of a very close friend. As active as he was, we were a little concerned about taking him, but we took that chance. It was a beautiful outdoor wedding at this gorgeous historic antebellum home in Mobile. We were so proud—he made it through the whole wedding without making a sound. Then came the closing prayer. The pastor began to pray, "God, we pray that your presence will be with . . ." and the minute Noah heard the word presence, he lifted up his head and loudly proclaimed, "Presents, I want presents!" Everyone around us snickered. It was so funny. Later on, when I was thinking about it, I thought, *isn't that the way we often do the Lord? We want His presents and all He can give us, but do not want to take time to be in His presence.* Many times, we have the attitude, "I want all you can give me Lord, but I don't have time to spend time with you." I pray we want the giver more than the gift.

Around the age of five, he wanted a Superman costume, so we had nothing else to do but go get him one. It was so sad when he put it on for the first time. He went running out of the house into the backyard with his arms outstretched straight to the sky. Much to his disappointment, nothing happened, but he tried it over and over again. It hurt my heart to see the disappointment on his face at the realization that he was not Superman, and he was not going to fly—that it was just a costume.

When he was around six years old, we were talking, and I made the comment that Jesus lives in my heart. Noah said "GG you know Jesus is too big to live in your heart. The Holy Spirit lives in your heart." I said, "You're exactly right."

Eden gave Noah the middle name, Christopher, after my brother Chris. Noah, just like my brother, loved Jesus. He's sweet like him, funny like him, and even somewhat favors him.

This was another sweet way of God showing his love to my family because my brother was in a car accident, hit head-on by a drunk driver, just as he started his senior year of Bible College in 1981. He never recovered from a massive brain injury and remained in a total vegetative state for the following eight years with a trach and feeding tube until he died in 1989.

There were many desperate cries and fasting for God to heal him. God doesn't always do things in the way we want or think He should. Believe me, I did not understand but I decided to trust and believe that God is a good, good Father. My brother is healed—not on earth as we planned—but in heaven. I miss him so much. But who would know such a beautiful gift from the Lord would come to us twenty-two years later through a little baby, Noah Christopher.

NOAH'S SALVATION AND BAPTISM

Nothing can make a GG happier than to see or hear about one of her grands giving their hearts to Jesus. Although we had dedicated Noah to the Lord as an infant, he had come to the realization that he needed to choose Jesus for himself. Noah was nine years old when he went to kids camp in the summer of 2021 with our church, City Hope.

He came home and told me that he gave his heart to Jesus. He said, "GG, I didn't go up to the front, but I asked Jesus into my heart." I said, "That's fine honey, you don't have to go to the front, you can get saved anywhere. You can talk to Jesus anywhere." I was overjoyed at this great news. I have always laid hands on Noah and prayed over him even when he sleeps, speaking God's favor and blessings over his life. Shortly after church camp, he asked if he could get baptized. Eden and I talked it over and felt like he needed to wait.

So, the next summer he went to church camp again. Soon after that, he again brought up the subject of getting baptized and said that he wanted to do it. Eden and I talked again and felt like he was ready, but we decided to at least take him

Noah's baptism

to the classes that our church has for anyone wanting to get baptized so that they can make sure they understand what it means. So, a few weeks later, I took him to the class. I felt like he answered the questions well that were asked and that he understood. The pastor asked the group, "Why do you want to get baptized?" "What does it mean?" Noah raised his hand and said, "To show the world that I love Jesus!" The pastor said, "Yes!" He then said, "If you have someone special in your life that you want to get in the baptismal tank with you, just let us know and we'll work that out." "Well," Noah said, "GG, I want you to go with me." I said okay, because to tell you the truth, you probably already know by now that I would do almost anything for that little boy, my honey from the rock. But I need to be honest, I instantly whispered, "Lord, you gotta help me out, because I just know I'm going to trip stepping into that tank and a tsunami is going to come over the top and soak everyone sitting on the front row!!" On Baptism Sunday they roll out these huge tanks full of water and put them pretty close to the front row.

The enemy tried to take Noah out before he was born. Glory to God for bringing Noah's mama out of drug addiction and saving his life.

Later on, I think it was that afternoon or the next day, God answered my prayer. We were riding in the car and Noah said, "GG, I want a man to baptize me, and Shane is the one. I know I'm not his real son, but he loves me like I am." As Noah would say, "It made my eyes water," instead of "It made me cry." It made me feel good to know he feels that way about Uncle Shane. Shane is a man Lindy met after getting out of jail. They spent a few more years in addiction. But I'm so thankful that they turned their lives over to Jesus, got sober in 2019, and got married. Sadly, Noah's dad is in prison and I pray all the time for godly men to step up in his life. We asked Uncle Shane and of course, he said he would be honored to do that with Noah and said, "I do love him like he's my son." The next thought I had was *thank ya Jesus, I'm not going to soak the front row.*

The next Sunday, May 22, 2022, was Baptism Day. Shane assisted in baptizing Noah. They had a little pre-baptism meeting that was held in a little back room before the service for people getting baptized. Shane told us later that he and Noah were the last two leaving the room, and the Pastor facilitating the baptism came up to Noah and said, "Noah, I want you to know that God has a plan and a purpose for your life. You have a call of God on your life. You're gonna be a mighty warrior for God." I was reminded of that verse: "What Satan intended for harm, God intended for good" (Genesis 15:20, author paraphrase). The enemy tried to take Noah out before he was born. Glory to God for bringing Noah's mama out of drug addiction and saving his life.

NOAH MEETS HIS DAD

When Noah was still fairly young, Eden was advised by a therapist to make a "picture book" with pictures showing different aspects of Donnie's life. It was to help Noah understand what "biological dad" means and to show pleasant stories about him. Eden also took Noah on a visit to meet his Dad when he was a little older.

They took money and were able to eat some snacks together and enjoy a little time, even if it was within the confines of those walls. Noah has a very tender heart and mentions at times that he feels sad for his Dad, sad that he has to be in prison, and wants us to pray for him. So, we hold hands and pray.

CHAPTER 16

No, Not the Feds Again!!!

... Do you want to be free from fear of the one in authority?
Then do what is right and you will be commended. For
the one in authority is God's servant for your good ...
—ROMANS 13:3-4

"PULL OVER!"

A few months after Noah was born, we were on our way to take him to his pediatrician for a check-up. We left our house that morning with Eden and Noah in her car, and I was following behind in my car. We took two cars that day because Eden had another appointment, and I was going to take Noah home with me after his doctor's check-up. We didn't even notice the feds were following us, of course, in two unmarked SUVs.

We only got about five miles away from our house when all of a sudden, one big black SUV pulled in front of Eden and one pulled directly behind me and boxed us in as they began to announce over their loudspeaker "Pull over, pull over now!" My heart was racing. I thought, *oh no, Eden must be going back to jail. This can't be happening.* Immediately, we pulled over and stopped in an open parking lot. They slowly walked up to our vehicles and asked if we had seen Greg P. I'm thinking, *these people are going to give me a heart attack.* The relief we felt was indescribable; I was so relieved that this time they were not after Eden. These were the same two federal marshals I had met that day nine months earlier at the motel Lindy and Eden were staying at. One of them was so kind. He said to Eden, "Can I just give you a hug?" "I am so proud of you; I rarely get to see the change in those I've arrested." Eden told him it was Jesus. As we got back into our cars, he said, "Let me know if you ever need anything." We got in our cars and headed to the doctor with Noah, thanking Jesus.

LUNCH WITH THE ARRESTING OFFICER

Several years later, in October 2020, Eden, Lindy, and I had the opportunity to take that same officer, Joseph G., to lunch at the Big Time Diner. At the time of the arrest in 2011, he was a corporal with the Mobile Police Department, assigned to the US Marshals as a Special Deputy US Marshal. We wanted to get his version of the events that took place back in 2011, as well as share with him the victories in our lives.

He remembered every detail of our story, although he could not share most of it. He brought up the picture of my girls that he had found when searching one of the rooms at the motel Lindy and Eden were staying at. He said it looked like they were at a wedding. He said they were so beautiful in that picture and he knew that on that day in 2011 when he had to put them in handcuffs and saw them sitting on that sidewalk, they didn't belong out there. We got to ask him why he pulled us over the day we were taking Noah to the pediatrician. I asked, "Why didn't you just come to our house and knock on our door to ask us that question, for goodness' sake!" He told us that he and the other officer were actually on their way to our house when they saw us pull out of the driveway that morning, so they followed us and pulled us over once we got a little way from our house. We told him how bad it scared us. We all laughed. He said it was so good to see the change in my daughters' lives and to know that, somehow, even if it was through an arrest, he played a part in it. I said, "That's exactly right, because God used that to turn them around." He told us that, sadly, he rarely gets to see this outcome."

It was such a relief to know Lindy and Eden were living right and did not need to fear those in authority.

EDEN'S PERSPECTIVE

My heart was pounding the day the officers boxed us in and pulled my mom and me over. My mind was racing with thoughts like, *I haven't done anything! Why are they pulling us over!?* They were looking for Greg P.

It was good just to be able to sit down with him and
share the rest of the story and the goodness of God.

I thought, oh my goodness, could there not have been an easier way to ask that simple question? I have to say, it was cool to see Officer G. again and know that he was encouraged by the change he saw in my life.

A few years later, we made arrangements to take him to lunch. Who goes to lunch with their arresting officer? Only my crazy family!! It was good just to be able to sit down with him and share the rest of the story and the goodness of God.

CHAPTER 17

Hope

And now these three remain: faith, hope and love.
—1 CORINTHIANS 13:13

SHARING OUR STORY

I remember one night sobbing in the middle of our mess saying, "Lord, this is only going to be worth it if you use this to help save lives, to give hope to others." I said, "If not, kill me now, because all of this will be in vain." In 2011, I saw God set Eden free and I'm so thankful to say that He has used our story to encourage and change others, but first, He used it to change me and Eden. Eden and I have been to several churches and rehabs to share our story, giving hope to others. It says in Revelation 12:11 (KJV), "And they overcame him by the blood of the Lamb and by the word of their testimony . . ." It is the life-giving message of the gospel of Jesus Christ reminding others to never give up, never stop praying, and never lose hope. Eden does not hesitate to share her story; it's so cool how the Holy Spirit just opens the door. She is a cosmetologist and has shared her story many times with people sitting in her chair while they get a haircut. God must have thought they needed a little more than a haircut that day when He picked her chair for them.

We have been through some really difficult times in our lives, but I refuse to be ashamed! Second Corinthians 5:17 (ESV, author paraphrase) tells me that if anyone is in Christ, he is a new creation. The old has gone, the new is here! The word "new" here translates in the Greek as "unused" or "unworn". I love it!! Brand new in Christ. God gives us a choice. I choose forgiveness, I choose grace and mercy, I choose freedom, and I choose Jesus!!

"Because of the Lord's great love we are not consumed, for His compassions never fail. They are new every morning; great is your faithfulness" (Lamentations 3:22-23). His mercies are new every morning!! To God be the Glory for our story!

RAISING UP INTERCESSORS

This is how awesome our God is. Many times, when we were in the middle of this darkness, I would cry out to God and ask Him to please send someone else to pray for my daughters. I don't know how to explain it other than I would just be exhausted, trying not to grow weary in the devastation.

Six years after God brought us through this mess, I was invited to speak at a Women's Conference, titled "Be Brave" in March 2017. The Conference was held in Mobile where most of the story in this book takes place. After I finished speaking and the conference had ended, this woman walked up to me and Eden and said to Eden, "I don't know who you are, but I prayed for you when all of this was going on." Neither of us had ever seen this woman before and we did not know her.

Faith is not seeing; it's knowing that you can absolutely depend on God.

She began to explain to us that as I was speaking and telling our testimony, she remembered her daughter asking her to pray for a girl named Eden. The woman went on to say that "she had a daughter in addiction at the same time as Eden." She told Eden who her daughter was, and Eden did remember her. She told us that while we were in the thick of it all, her daughter came home to see her one day and said to her "Mom, there's this girl, her name is Eden; she just doesn't belong out there, she's different. I want you to pray for her." The woman told us that she began to pray for Eden.

We all stood there with tears in awe at the goodness of our God! God raised this woman up whom we had never met to help pray for Eden, even when we didn't know it. When we ask God for help, we need to trust that He is doing it. Even when we don't see or feel that He's working. He never stops working. Faith is not seeing; it's knowing that you can absolutely depend on God. I can't even tell you the blessing I felt that day when God smiled down on us. What were the chances we would ever meet this woman and that she would show up at a conference where she would hear our whole story? Only God could line this up.

STILL KICKIN' IT FOR JESUS

Eden loves Jesus and she loves to sing. She prefers singing over public speaking—not me—I prefer public speaking over singing; that's probably because she can sing really well and I can't. The Lord did not give me that talent. I sure wish He had, but if He had, I'd probably be dealing with pride again.

Eden has sung at churches, funerals, and several rehabs where we have shared our story. I tried to sing a few times in my younger days, but let's just say that's not my gift. A close friend of mine asked me to sing at her husband's funeral. Many, many years had passed since she had heard me sing and I guess she just didn't remember that I really can't, but I didn't want to let her down in such a time of grief. So, I said yes and immediately called Eden and said, "Please, you have to go with me." So she did, and we sang a duet.

Afterward, this elderly man came up to me and said, "Your daughter can really sing, but you, ummm . . . not so much." I laughed and thought, sometimes, you just gotta accept the things you cannot change.

My beautiful daughter, Eden, who was once bound by the chains of drug addiction, feeling hopeless, is now center stage, singing praises to the one who deserves all the glory—His name is Jesus. And I get to look up and see it. My mind goes back to that Sunday when she was four years old on stage in that little Methodist Church with her sisters, kicking her leg up and singing her heart out, "He's Still Working On Me." The truth is, He's still working on all of us until we meet Him face to face. Today, she is drug-free and back to kickin' it for Jesus!

He did it for me. He will do it for you.

EDEN'S MESSAGE: NEVER GIVE UP

The feeling of hopelessness is very devastating. It is only by the Grace of God that I am still here. I am truly an example that He leaves the ninety-nine to come after that one lost sheep.

> *Suppose one of you has a hundred sheep and loses one of them. Doesn't he leave the ninety-nine in the open country and go after the lost sheep until he finds it? And when he finds it, he joyfully puts it on his shoulders and goes home."—Luke 15:3-6*

I am blown away by the love of God to save me and my son. It was so cool to meet Mrs. H. at the Women's Conference and to hear her story of how she prayed for a girl named "Eden" that she didn't even know. When God calls you to pray for someone, be committed and pray. You could be saving a life. I'm overwhelmed by the goodness of God. He did it for me. He will do it for you. My prayer is that our story brings hope and freedom to many others.

Printed in the USA
CPSIA information can be obtained
at www.ICGtesting.com
LVHW020556081123
763363LV00050B/247

9 781960 678911